60 Baking Recipes for Home

By: Kelly Johnson

Table of Contents

Breads and Rolls:
- Classic French Baguette
- Whole Wheat Sourdough Bread
- Cinnamon Raisin Bread
- Garlic and Herb Focaccia
- Soft Pretzels
- Cheddar and Jalapeño Cornbread
- Rosemary Olive Oil Bread
- Pumpkin Bread
- Hawaiian Sweet Rolls
- Pesto Swirl Bread

Muffins and Cupcakes:
- Blueberry Muffins
- Chocolate Chip Banana Muffins
- Lemon Poppy Seed Muffins
- Red Velvet Cupcakes
- Raspberry Almond Cupcakes
- Carrot Cake Muffins
- Maple Pecan Muffins
- Double Chocolate Zucchini Muffins
- Orange Cranberry Muffins
- Snickerdoodle Cupcakes

Breads and Rolls:
- Chocolate Chip Cookies
- Oatmeal Raisin Cookies
- Peanut Butter Blossoms
- White Chocolate Macadamia Nut Cookies
- Double Chocolate Mint Cookies
- Almond Butter Cookies
- Lemon Shortbread Cookies
- Coconut Macaroons
- Espresso Chocolate Chunk Cookies

- Pistachio Cranberry Biscotti

Pastries and Tarts:

- Apple Turnovers
- Strawberry Danish
- Chocolate Croissants (Pain au Chocolat)
- Mixed Berry Galette
- Lemon Tart
- Nutella Pastry Twists
- Raspberry Linzer Cookies
- Baklava
- Mini Quiches
- Pecan Pie Bars

Cakes:

- Classic Vanilla Cake
- Chocolate Layer Cake
- Lemon Blueberry Bundt Cake
- Carrot Cake with Cream Cheese Frosting
- Almond Joy Cake
- Red Wine Chocolate Cake
- Tiramisu Cake
- Pineapple Upside-Down Cake
- Coconut Lime Pound Cake
- Black Forest Cake
-

Gluten-Free and Vegan Options:
- Gluten-Free Chocolate Chip Cookies
- Vegan Banana Bread
- Gluten-Free Lemon Bars
- Vegan Chocolate Cupcakes
- Almond Flour Brownies (Gluten-Free)
- Vegan Blueberry Scones
- Gluten-Free Pumpkin Muffins
- Vegan Chocolate Avocado Cake
- Coconut Flour Pancakes (Gluten-Free)
- Vegan Almond Joy Energy Bites

Breads and Rolls:

Classic French Baguette

Ingredients:

- 4 cups all-purpose flour
- 1 tablespoon active dry yeast
- 1 1/2 teaspoons salt
- 1 1/2 cups warm water (about 110°F/43°C)

Instructions:

Activate the Yeast:
- In a small bowl, combine the warm water and yeast. Let it sit for about 5-10 minutes until the mixture becomes frothy.

Combine Ingredients:
- In a large mixing bowl, combine the flour and salt. Create a well in the center and pour in the activated yeast mixture.

Knead the Dough:
- Gradually incorporate the flour into the wet ingredients until a dough forms. Turn the dough onto a floured surface and knead for about 8-10 minutes until it becomes smooth and elastic.

First Rise:
- Place the dough in a lightly oiled bowl, cover it with a clean kitchen towel, and let it rise in a warm place for 1-2 hours or until it doubles in size.

Shape the Baguette:
- Preheat your oven to 450°F (230°C). Punch down the risen dough and turn it onto a floured surface. Divide it into two equal parts and shape each into a baguette. Place them on a parchment-lined baking sheet.

Second Rise:
- Cover the shaped baguettes with a kitchen towel and let them rise for another 30-45 minutes.

Score the Baguettes:
- Using a sharp knife or a razor blade, make diagonal slashes along the tops of the baguettes.

Bake:
- Bake in the preheated oven for 20-25 minutes or until the baguettes are golden brown and sound hollow when tapped.

Cool:
- Allow the baguettes to cool on a wire rack before slicing.

Tips:

- For a crispy crust, you can mist the oven with water just before placing the baguettes inside.
- You can also place a pan of water on the bottom rack of the oven to create steam, enhancing the crust.
- Experiment with different flours for variations in flavor and texture.

Enjoy your homemade classic French baguette!

Whole Wheat Sourdough Bread

Ingredients:

- 1 cup active sourdough starter
- 1 1/2 cups lukewarm water
- 3 1/2 cups whole wheat flour
- 1 1/2 teaspoons salt
- 1 tablespoon honey or maple syrup (optional, for a touch of sweetness)

Instructions:

Activate the Starter:
- In a large mixing bowl, combine the active sourdough starter, lukewarm water, and honey or maple syrup if using. Mix well.

Add Flour and Salt:
- Gradually add the whole wheat flour and salt to the mixture. Stir until a shaggy dough forms.

Knead the Dough:
- Turn the dough out onto a floured surface and knead for about 10-15 minutes until it becomes smooth and elastic. Add more flour if the dough is too sticky.

First Rise:
- Place the kneaded dough in a lightly oiled bowl, cover it with a damp cloth, and let it rise in a warm place for 4-8 hours or until it doubles in size. This is the bulk fermentation stage.

Shape the Loaf:
- Turn the dough onto a floured surface and shape it into a round or oval loaf. Place the shaped dough in a well-floured proofing basket or bowl, seam side down.

Second Rise:
- Cover the shaped loaf with a kitchen towel and let it rise for an additional 2-4 hours or until it visibly expands and passes the poke test.

Preheat the Oven:
- Preheat your oven to 450°F (230°C) with a lidded Dutch oven inside.

Score the Loaf:
- Just before baking, score the surface of the loaf with a sharp knife or razor blade to allow for controlled expansion.

Bake in the Dutch Oven:
- Carefully transfer the scored dough into the preheated Dutch oven. Cover with the lid and bake for 20 minutes.

Uncover and Finish Baking:
- Remove the lid and continue baking for an additional 20-25 minutes or until the crust is golden brown and the bread sounds hollow when tapped.

Cool:
- Allow the sourdough bread to cool on a wire rack before slicing.

Tips:

- Adjust the fermentation time based on the temperature in your kitchen. Warmer environments may require less time.
- You can experiment with adding seeds or nuts to the dough for added flavor and texture.

Enjoy your wholesome homemade whole wheat sourdough bread!

Cinnamon Raisin Bread

Ingredients:

- 1 cup warm milk (about 110°F/43°C)
- 2 1/4 teaspoons active dry yeast
- 1/4 cup granulated sugar
- 3 1/2 cups all-purpose flour
- 1 teaspoon salt
- 2 teaspoons ground cinnamon
- 1 large egg
- 1/4 cup unsalted butter, softened
- 1 cup raisins

For the Filling:

- 1/4 cup unsalted butter, melted
- 1/2 cup brown sugar
- 2 teaspoons ground cinnamon

Instructions:

Activate the Yeast:
- In a small bowl, combine warm milk, active dry yeast, and a pinch of sugar. Let it sit for 5-10 minutes until frothy.

Make the Dough:
- In a large mixing bowl, combine the activated yeast mixture, sugar, flour, salt, ground cinnamon, egg, and softened butter. Mix until a dough forms.

Knead the Dough:
- Turn the dough onto a floured surface and knead for about 8-10 minutes until it becomes smooth and elastic.

First Rise:
- Place the dough in a lightly oiled bowl, cover it with a damp cloth, and let it rise in a warm place for 1-2 hours or until it doubles in size.

Prepare the Filling:
- In a small bowl, mix together melted butter, brown sugar, and ground cinnamon to create the filling.

Roll and Fill:

- Turn the risen dough onto a floured surface and roll it into a rectangle. Spread the filling evenly over the surface, then sprinkle raisins on top.

Shape and Second Rise:
- Roll the dough tightly from one end to the other, forming a log. Place the log into a greased loaf pan and let it rise for an additional 1-2 hours.

Preheat the Oven:
- Preheat your oven to 350°F (180°C).

Bake:
- Bake the cinnamon raisin bread in the preheated oven for 30-35 minutes or until golden brown and cooked through. You can cover it with foil if the top is browning too quickly.

Cool:
- Allow the bread to cool in the pan for 10 minutes, then transfer it to a wire rack to cool completely before slicing.

Tips:

- For extra flavor, add a dash of vanilla extract to the dough or sprinkle chopped nuts along with the raisins.
- Enjoy toasted with butter or cream cheese.

Enjoy your homemade cinnamon raisin bread!

Garlic and Herb Focaccia

Ingredients:

For the Dough:

- 4 cups all-purpose flour
- 1 tablespoon sugar
- 1 tablespoon active dry yeast
- 1 1/2 teaspoons salt
- 1 1/2 cups warm water (about 110°F/43°C)
- 1/4 cup olive oil

For the Topping:

- 1/4 cup olive oil
- 4 cloves garlic, minced
- 1 tablespoon fresh rosemary, chopped
- 1 tablespoon fresh thyme leaves
- Coarse sea salt for sprinkling

Instructions:

Activate the Yeast:
- In a small bowl, combine warm water, sugar, and active dry yeast. Let it sit for 5-10 minutes until it becomes frothy.

Make the Dough:
- In a large mixing bowl, combine the flour and salt. Make a well in the center and pour in the activated yeast mixture and olive oil. Mix until a dough forms.

Knead the Dough:
- Turn the dough onto a floured surface and knead for about 8-10 minutes until it becomes smooth and elastic.

First Rise:
- Place the dough in a lightly oiled bowl, cover it with a damp cloth, and let it rise in a warm place for 1-2 hours or until it doubles in size.

Preheat the Oven:

- Preheat your oven to 425°F (220°C).

Shape the Focaccia:
- Punch down the risen dough and transfer it to a parchment-lined baking sheet. Press the dough evenly into a rectangle or circle.

Second Rise:
- Cover the shaped dough with a damp cloth and let it rise for an additional 30-45 minutes.

Make indentations:
- Use your fingers to make deep indentations all over the surface of the dough.

Prepare the Topping:
- In a small bowl, mix together olive oil, minced garlic, rosemary, and thyme.

Top the Focaccia:
- Brush the olive oil and herb mixture evenly over the surface of the dough. Sprinkle with coarse sea salt.

Bake:
- Bake in the preheated oven for 20-25 minutes or until the focaccia is golden brown and sounds hollow when tapped.

Cool:
- Allow the garlic and herb focaccia to cool on a wire rack before slicing.

Tips:

- Customize the herbs to your preference; basil and oregano also work well.
- Serve with a side of balsamic vinegar and olive oil for dipping.

Enjoy your aromatic garlic and herb focaccia!

Soft Pretzels

Ingredients:

For the Dough:

- 1 1/2 cups warm water (about 110°F/43°C)
- 1 tablespoon sugar
- 2 teaspoons active dry yeast
- 4 1/2 cups all-purpose flour
- 1 1/2 teaspoons salt

For the Baking Soda Bath:

- 10 cups water
- 2/3 cup baking soda

For Topping:

- Coarse salt
- Melted butter for brushing (optional)

Instructions:

- Activate the Yeast:
    - In a bowl, combine warm water, sugar, and active dry yeast. Let it sit for 5-10 minutes until frothy.
- Make the Dough:
    - In a large mixing bowl, combine the flour and salt. Make a well in the center and pour in the activated yeast mixture. Mix until a dough forms.
- Knead the Dough:
    - Turn the dough onto a floured surface and knead for about 5-7 minutes until it becomes smooth and elastic.
- First Rise:
    - Place the dough in a lightly oiled bowl, cover it with a damp cloth, and let it rise in a warm place for 1 hour or until it doubles in size.
- Preheat the Oven:
    - Preheat your oven to 450°F (230°C).
- Prepare Baking Soda Bath:

- In a large, wide pot, bring 10 cups of water to a boil. Carefully add baking soda to the boiling water.

Shape the Pretzels:
- Divide the risen dough into 8 equal portions. Roll each portion into a long rope and shape it into a pretzel.

Boil the Pretzels:
- Gently place each pretzel into the boiling water for about 30 seconds, flipping once. Remove with a slotted spoon and place on a parchment-lined baking sheet.

Topping and Baking:
- Sprinkle coarse salt over the pretzels. Bake in the preheated oven for 10-12 minutes or until they turn golden brown.

Optional: Brush with Butter:
- Optional: Brush the baked pretzels with melted butter for a shiny finish.

Cool:
- Allow the soft pretzels to cool on a wire rack for a few minutes before serving.

Tips:

- Customize the toppings by adding sesame seeds, poppy seeds, or grated cheese.
- Serve with your favorite mustard or cheese dip.

Enjoy your homemade soft pretzels – perfect for snacking or game day!

Cheddar and Jalapeño Cornbread

Ingredients:

- 1 cup cornmeal
- 1 cup all-purpose flour
- 1 tablespoon baking powder
- 1 teaspoon salt
- 1 cup buttermilk
- 2 large eggs
- 1/4 cup unsalted butter, melted
- 1 cup shredded cheddar cheese
- 2-3 jalapeños, seeded and finely chopped

Instructions:

Preheat the Oven:
- Preheat your oven to 400°F (200°C). Grease a square baking pan (8 or 9 inches) or use parchment paper.

Mix Dry Ingredients:
- In a large mixing bowl, combine the cornmeal, all-purpose flour, baking powder, and salt.

Prepare Wet Ingredients:
- In a separate bowl, whisk together buttermilk, eggs, and melted butter.

Combine Wet and Dry Ingredients:
- Pour the wet ingredients into the dry ingredients and stir until just combined. Do not overmix; a few lumps are okay.

Add Cheese and Jalapeños:
- Gently fold in the shredded cheddar cheese and chopped jalapeños into the batter.

Bake:
- Pour the batter into the prepared baking pan, spreading it evenly. Bake in the preheated oven for 20-25 minutes or until the edges are golden brown and a toothpick inserted into the center comes out clean.

Cool:
- Allow the cheddar and jalapeño cornbread to cool in the pan for 10 minutes, then transfer it to a wire rack.

Slice and Serve:

- Once cooled, slice the cornbread into squares or wedges and serve.

Tips:

- Adjust the amount of jalapeños based on your spice preference.
- For an extra kick, you can add a pinch of cayenne pepper to the dry ingredients.
- Serve with honey or butter for added flavor.

Enjoy this savory and slightly spicy Cheddar and Jalapeño Cornbread as a side dish for chili, soups, or barbecue!

Rosemary Olive Oil Bread

Ingredients:

- 3 1/2 cups all-purpose flour
- 1 packet (2 1/4 teaspoons) active dry yeast
- 1 1/2 teaspoons salt
- 1 1/4 cups warm water (about 110°F/43°C)
- 2 tablespoons fresh rosemary, finely chopped
- 1/4 cup extra virgin olive oil
- 1 tablespoon honey
- 1/2 cup Kalamata olives, pitted and chopped

Instructions:

Activate the Yeast:
- In a small bowl, combine warm water and honey. Sprinkle the yeast over the water and let it sit for 5-10 minutes until it becomes frothy.

Mix Dry Ingredients:
- In a large mixing bowl, combine the flour and salt. Make a well in the center.

Combine Wet Ingredients:
- Pour the activated yeast mixture, olive oil, and chopped rosemary into the well. Mix until a dough forms.

Knead the Dough:
- Turn the dough onto a floured surface and knead for about 8-10 minutes until it becomes smooth and elastic.

First Rise:
- Place the kneaded dough in a lightly oiled bowl, cover it with a damp cloth, and let it rise in a warm place for 1-2 hours or until it doubles in size.

Add Olives:
- Punch down the risen dough and knead in the chopped olives until evenly distributed.

Shape the Loaf:
- Shape the dough into a round or oval loaf and place it on a parchment-lined baking sheet.

Second Rise:
- Cover the shaped loaf with a damp cloth and let it rise for an additional 30-45 minutes.

Preheat the Oven:
- Preheat your oven to 375°F (190°C).

Bake:
- Bake the rosemary olive oil bread in the preheated oven for 25-30 minutes or until it is golden brown and sounds hollow when tapped.

Cool:
- Allow the bread to cool on a wire rack before slicing.

Tips:

- You can brush the top of the bread with extra olive oil before baking for a shiny finish.
- Experiment with different varieties of olives for unique flavors.
- Serve with a balsamic dipping sauce or olive tapenade.

Enjoy your aromatic Rosemary Olive Oil Bread, perfect for serving with soups, salads, or as a delightful snack!

Pumpkin Bread

Ingredients:

- 1 3/4 cups all-purpose flour
- 1 teaspoon baking soda
- 1/2 teaspoon baking powder
- 1/2 teaspoon salt
- 1 teaspoon ground cinnamon
- 1/2 teaspoon ground nutmeg
- 1/2 teaspoon ground cloves
- 1/4 teaspoon ground ginger
- 1/2 cup unsalted butter, softened
- 1 cup granulated sugar
- 1/2 cup packed brown sugar
- 2 large eggs
- 1 cup canned pumpkin puree
- 1/3 cup water
- 1 teaspoon vanilla extract
- 1/2 cup chopped nuts (optional)

Instructions:

Preheat the Oven:
- Preheat your oven to 350°F (175°C). Grease and flour a 9x5-inch loaf pan.

Mix Dry Ingredients:
- In a medium bowl, whisk together the flour, baking soda, baking powder, salt, cinnamon, nutmeg, cloves, and ginger. Set aside.

Cream Butter and Sugars:
- In a large mixing bowl, cream together the softened butter, granulated sugar, and brown sugar until light and fluffy.

Add Eggs and Pumpkin:
- Beat in the eggs one at a time, then mix in the pumpkin puree.

Combine Wet and Dry Ingredients:
- Gradually add the dry ingredients to the wet ingredients, mixing just until combined. Add water and vanilla extract, and continue to mix until smooth.

Optional: Add Nuts:
- If desired, fold in chopped nuts into the batter.

Pour into Pan:
- Pour the batter into the prepared loaf pan, spreading it evenly.

Bake:
- Bake in the preheated oven for 60-70 minutes or until a toothpick inserted into the center comes out clean.

Cool:
- Allow the pumpkin bread to cool in the pan for 10 minutes, then transfer it to a wire rack to cool completely.

Tips:

- Adjust the spices to your preference; you can also add a pinch of allspice or cardamom for extra flavor.
- Consider adding chocolate chips or raisins for a variation.
- Store the pumpkin bread in an airtight container to keep it moist.

Enjoy your delicious homemade Pumpkin Bread, perfect for autumn or any time of the year!

Hawaiian Sweet Rolls

Ingredients:

For the Rolls:

- 3/4 cup pineapple juice (room temperature)
- 1/2 cup unsalted butter, melted
- 1/2 cup granulated sugar
- 2 large eggs
- 4 1/2 cups all-purpose flour
- 1 teaspoon salt
- 2 1/4 teaspoons active dry yeast

For the Glaze:

- 1/4 cup unsalted butter, melted
- 2 tablespoons honey

Instructions:

Activate the Yeast:
- In a small bowl, combine the pineapple juice and yeast. Let it sit for 5-10 minutes until frothy.

Mix Wet Ingredients:
- In a large mixing bowl, whisk together the melted butter, sugar, and eggs. Add the activated yeast mixture and mix well.

Combine Dry Ingredients:
- In another bowl, whisk together the flour and salt.

Make the Dough:
- Gradually add the dry ingredients to the wet ingredients, stirring continuously, until a soft dough forms.

Knead the Dough:
- Turn the dough onto a floured surface and knead for about 8-10 minutes until it becomes smooth and elastic.

First Rise:
- Place the dough in a lightly oiled bowl, cover it with a damp cloth, and let it rise in a warm place for 1-2 hours or until it doubles in size.

Shape the Rolls:

- Punch down the risen dough and divide it into 15-18 equal portions. Shape each portion into a ball and place them close together in a greased baking dish.

Second Rise:
- Cover the shaped rolls with a damp cloth and let them rise for an additional 30-45 minutes.

Preheat the Oven:
- Preheat your oven to 350°F (175°C).

Bake:
- Bake the Hawaiian sweet rolls in the preheated oven for 15-20 minutes or until they are golden brown.

Prepare the Glaze:
- In a small bowl, mix together the melted butter and honey.

Glaze the Rolls:
- Once the rolls are out of the oven, brush them with the honey-butter glaze while they are still warm.

Cool:
- Allow the Hawaiian sweet rolls to cool in the baking dish for a few minutes before transferring them to a wire rack.

Tips:

- You can add a touch of coconut extract for an extra hint of Hawaiian flavor.
- Serve the rolls with your favorite tropical jam or as a side to a savory dish.

Enjoy your delightful homemade Hawaiian Sweet Rolls!

Pesto Swirl Bread

Ingredients:

For the Bread:

- 3 1/2 cups all-purpose flour
- 1 tablespoon sugar
- 1 teaspoon salt
- 2 1/4 teaspoons active dry yeast
- 1 cup warm milk (about 110°F/43°C)
- 2 tablespoons unsalted butter, melted
- 1/4 cup pesto sauce (store-bought or homemade)

For the Pesto:

- 2 cups fresh basil leaves, packed
- 1/2 cup freshly grated Parmesan cheese
- 1/2 cup pine nuts or walnuts
- 2 cloves garlic
- 1/2 cup extra virgin olive oil
- Salt and pepper to taste

Instructions:

For the Pesto:

    Prepare the Pesto:
- In a food processor, combine basil, Parmesan cheese, pine nuts or walnuts, and garlic. Pulse until finely chopped.

    Add Olive Oil:
- With the food processor running, gradually add the olive oil in a steady stream until the pesto reaches a smooth consistency. Season with salt and pepper to taste. Set aside.

For the Bread:

    Activate the Yeast:
- In a small bowl, combine warm milk and sugar. Sprinkle the yeast over the milk and let it sit for 5-10 minutes until frothy.

Mix Dry Ingredients:
- In a large mixing bowl, whisk together the flour and salt.

Combine Wet and Dry Ingredients:
- Make a well in the center of the flour mixture. Pour the activated yeast mixture and melted butter into the well. Mix until a dough forms.

Knead the Dough:
- Turn the dough onto a floured surface and knead for about 8-10 minutes until it becomes smooth and elastic.

First Rise:
- Place the dough in a lightly oiled bowl, cover it with a damp cloth, and let it rise in a warm place for 1-2 hours or until it doubles in size.

Prepare the Pesto Swirl:
- Punch down the risen dough and roll it out into a rectangle. Spread the pesto evenly over the surface of the dough.

Roll and Shape:
- Roll up the dough tightly from one end to the other, forming a log. Place the log into a greased loaf pan.

Second Rise:
- Cover the loaf pan with a damp cloth and let it rise for an additional 30-45 minutes.

Preheat the Oven:
- Preheat your oven to 375°F (190°C).

Bake:
- Bake the pesto swirl bread in the preheated oven for 25-30 minutes or until it is golden brown and sounds hollow when tapped.

Cool:
- Allow the bread to cool in the pan for 10 minutes, then transfer it to a wire rack to cool completely.

Tips:

- Adjust the amount of pesto according to your taste preferences.
- Experiment with different types of nuts in the pesto for added flavor variations.

Enjoy your delightful Pesto Swirl Bread, perfect for serving as a unique and flavorful side!

Muffins and Cupcakes:
Blueberry Muffins

Ingredients:

- 2 cups all-purpose flour
- 1 tablespoon baking powder
- 1/2 teaspoon baking soda
- 1/4 teaspoon salt
- 1/2 cup unsalted butter, softened
- 1 cup granulated sugar
- 2 large eggs
- 1 teaspoon vanilla extract
- 1 cup buttermilk
- 1 1/2 cups fresh or frozen blueberries (if using frozen, do not thaw)

For Streusel Topping (optional):

- 1/4 cup all-purpose flour
- 2 tablespoons granulated sugar
- 2 tablespoons cold unsalted butter, cut into small pieces

Instructions:

Preheat the Oven:
- Preheat your oven to 375°F (190°C). Line a muffin tin with paper liners or grease the cups.

Prepare Streusel Topping (Optional):
- In a small bowl, combine flour, sugar, and cold butter pieces. Use a fork or your fingers to mix until crumbly. Set aside.

Mix Dry Ingredients:
- In a medium bowl, whisk together the flour, baking powder, baking soda, and salt. Set aside.

Cream Butter and Sugar:
- In a large mixing bowl, cream together the softened butter and sugar until light and fluffy.

Add Eggs and Vanilla:
- Beat in the eggs one at a time, then mix in the vanilla extract.

Alternate Dry and Wet Ingredients:

- Gradually add the dry ingredients to the wet ingredients, alternating with the buttermilk. Begin and end with the dry ingredients. Mix until just combined.

Fold in Blueberries:
- Gently fold in the blueberries until evenly distributed throughout the batter.

Fill Muffin Cups:
- Divide the batter evenly among the muffin cups, filling each about 2/3 full.

Add Streusel Topping (Optional):
- If using streusel topping, sprinkle it over the muffin batter in each cup.

Bake:
- Bake in the preheated oven for 18-22 minutes or until a toothpick inserted into the center of a muffin comes out clean.

Cool:
- Allow the blueberry muffins to cool in the muffin tin for a few minutes before transferring them to a wire rack to cool completely.

Tips:

- If using frozen blueberries, toss them in a bit of flour before folding them into the batter to prevent them from sinking to the bottom.
- For added flavor, consider adding a pinch of lemon zest to the batter.

Enjoy your delicious homemade Blueberry Muffins!

Chocolate Chip Banana Muffins

Ingredients:

- 2 to 3 ripe bananas, mashed (about 1 cup)
- 1/3 cup melted unsalted butter
- 1 teaspoon baking soda
- Pinch of salt
- 3/4 cup granulated sugar
- 1 large egg, beaten
- 1 teaspoon vanilla extract
- 1 1/2 cups all-purpose flour
- 1 cup chocolate chips

Instructions:

Preheat the Oven:
- Preheat your oven to 350°F (175°C). Line a muffin tin with paper liners or grease the cups.

Mash Bananas:
- In a mixing bowl, mash the ripe bananas with a fork or potato masher.

Add Melted Butter:
- Stir the melted butter into the mashed bananas.

Add Baking Soda and Salt:
- Add the baking soda and a pinch of salt to the banana mixture. Stir to combine.

Add Sugar, Beaten Egg, and Vanilla:
- Mix in the granulated sugar, beaten egg, and vanilla extract.

Add Flour:
- Gently fold in the flour until just combined. Be careful not to overmix; a few lumps are okay.

Fold in Chocolate Chips:
- Gently fold in the chocolate chips until evenly distributed throughout the batter.

Fill Muffin Cups:
- Divide the batter evenly among the muffin cups, filling each about 2/3 full.

Bake:

- Bake in the preheated oven for 18-20 minutes or until a toothpick inserted into the center of a muffin comes out clean.

Cool:
- Allow the chocolate chip banana muffins to cool in the muffin tin for a few minutes before transferring them to a wire rack to cool completely.

Tips:

- If your bananas aren't quite ripe, you can enhance their sweetness by placing them in the oven at 300°F (150°C) for 15-20 minutes until the skins turn black.
- Consider adding chopped nuts or a sprinkle of cinnamon to the batter for extra flavor.

Enjoy these delicious Chocolate Chip Banana Muffins as a delightful treat or a quick breakfast option!

Lemon Poppy Seed Muffins

Ingredients:

- 2 cups all-purpose flour
- 2 tablespoons poppy seeds
- 1 teaspoon baking powder
- 1/2 teaspoon baking soda
- 1/4 teaspoon salt
- 1/2 cup unsalted butter, softened
- 1 cup granulated sugar
- 2 large eggs
- 1 teaspoon vanilla extract
- 1 tablespoon lemon zest (from about 2 lemons)
- 1/4 cup fresh lemon juice (from about 2 lemons)
- 1 cup buttermilk

For the Glaze:

- 1 cup powdered sugar
- 2 tablespoons fresh lemon juice

Instructions:

Preheat the Oven:
- Preheat your oven to 375°F (190°C). Line a muffin tin with paper liners or grease the cups.

Mix Dry Ingredients:
- In a medium bowl, whisk together the flour, poppy seeds, baking powder, baking soda, and salt. Set aside.

Cream Butter and Sugar:
- In a large mixing bowl, cream together the softened butter and granulated sugar until light and fluffy.

Add Eggs and Vanilla:
- Beat in the eggs one at a time, then mix in the vanilla extract.

Add Lemon Zest and Juice:
- Stir in the lemon zest and fresh lemon juice.

Alternate Dry and Wet Ingredients:

- Gradually add the dry ingredients to the wet ingredients, alternating with the buttermilk. Begin and end with the dry ingredients. Mix until just combined.

Fill Muffin Cups:
- Divide the batter evenly among the muffin cups, filling each about 2/3 full.

Bake:
- Bake in the preheated oven for 18-20 minutes or until a toothpick inserted into the center of a muffin comes out clean.

Cool:
- Allow the lemon poppy seed muffins to cool in the muffin tin for a few minutes before transferring them to a wire rack to cool completely.

For the Glaze:

Prepare Glaze:
- In a small bowl, whisk together the powdered sugar and fresh lemon juice until smooth.

Drizzle Glaze:
- Drizzle the glaze over the cooled muffins.

Tips:

- Adjust the amount of lemon zest and juice according to your taste preferences.
- For a richer flavor, consider adding a touch of almond extract to the batter.

Enjoy these zesty and delightful Lemon Poppy Seed Muffins!

Red Velvet Cupcakes

Ingredients:

For the Cupcakes:

- 2 1/2 cups all-purpose flour
- 1 1/2 cups granulated sugar
- 1 teaspoon baking powder
- 1 teaspoon baking soda
- 1/2 teaspoon salt
- 2 tablespoons cocoa powder
- 1 1/2 cups vegetable oil
- 1 cup buttermilk, room temperature
- 2 large eggs, room temperature
- 2 tablespoons red food coloring
- 1 teaspoon vanilla extract
- 1 teaspoon white vinegar or apple cider vinegar

For the Cream Cheese Frosting:

- 8 ounces cream cheese, softened
- 1/2 cup unsalted butter, softened
- 4 cups powdered sugar
- 1 teaspoon vanilla extract

Instructions:

For the Cupcakes:

Preheat the Oven:
- Preheat your oven to 350°F (175°C). Line a muffin tin with cupcake liners.

Mix Dry Ingredients:
- In a large bowl, whisk together the flour, sugar, baking powder, baking soda, salt, and cocoa powder.

Combine Wet Ingredients:
- In a separate bowl, whisk together the vegetable oil, buttermilk, eggs, red food coloring, vanilla extract, and vinegar.

Mix Wet and Dry Ingredients:

- Gradually add the wet ingredients to the dry ingredients, mixing until just combined. Be careful not to overmix.

Fill Cupcake Liners:
- Divide the batter evenly among the cupcake liners, filling each about 2/3 full.

Bake:
- Bake in the preheated oven for 18-20 minutes or until a toothpick inserted into the center of a cupcake comes out clean.

Cool:
- Allow the red velvet cupcakes to cool in the muffin tin for a few minutes, then transfer them to a wire rack to cool completely.

For the Cream Cheese Frosting:

Prepare Frosting:
- In a mixing bowl, beat the softened cream cheese and butter until smooth and creamy.

Add Powdered Sugar and Vanilla:
- Gradually add the powdered sugar, one cup at a time, and beat until well combined. Add the vanilla extract and beat until fluffy.

Frost Cupcakes:
- Once the cupcakes are completely cooled, frost them with the cream cheese frosting using a piping bag or a spatula.

Optional: Decorate:
- Decorate with additional red velvet crumbs, sprinkles, or a drizzle of chocolate if desired.

Tips:

- Ensure that the buttermilk, eggs, and butter are at room temperature for a smoother batter.
- Adjust the amount of red food coloring based on your desired intensity.

Enjoy these classic Red Velvet Cupcakes with creamy cream cheese frosting!

Raspberry Almond Cupcakes

Ingredients:

For the Cupcakes:

- 1 1/2 cups all-purpose flour
- 1 1/2 teaspoons baking powder
- 1/4 teaspoon salt
- 1/2 cup unsalted butter, softened
- 1 cup granulated sugar
- 2 large eggs
- 1 teaspoon almond extract
- 1/2 cup whole milk
- 1/2 cup fresh raspberries, chopped

For the Almond Frosting:

- 1 cup unsalted butter, softened
- 4 cups powdered sugar
- 1 teaspoon almond extract
- 2-3 tablespoons milk
- Sliced almonds for garnish

Instructions:

For the Cupcakes:

Preheat the Oven:
- Preheat your oven to 350°F (175°C). Line a muffin tin with cupcake liners.

Mix Dry Ingredients:
- In a medium bowl, whisk together the flour, baking powder, and salt. Set aside.

Cream Butter and Sugar:
- In a large mixing bowl, cream together the softened butter and sugar until light and fluffy.

Add Eggs and Almond Extract:
- Beat in the eggs one at a time, then mix in the almond extract.

Alternate Dry and Wet Ingredients:

- Gradually add the dry ingredients to the wet ingredients, alternating with the milk. Begin and end with the dry ingredients. Mix until just combined.

Fold in Raspberries:
- Gently fold in the chopped raspberries until evenly distributed throughout the batter.

Fill Cupcake Liners:
- Divide the batter evenly among the cupcake liners, filling each about 2/3 full.

Bake:
- Bake in the preheated oven for 18-20 minutes or until a toothpick inserted into the center of a cupcake comes out clean.

Cool:
- Allow the raspberry almond cupcakes to cool in the muffin tin for a few minutes, then transfer them to a wire rack to cool completely.

For the Almond Frosting:

Prepare Frosting:
- In a mixing bowl, beat the softened butter until creamy.

Add Powdered Sugar and Almond Extract:
- Gradually add the powdered sugar, one cup at a time, and beat until well combined. Add the almond extract and continue to beat until fluffy.

Adjust Consistency:
- If the frosting is too thick, add milk, one tablespoon at a time, until you reach your desired consistency.

Frost Cupcakes:
- Once the cupcakes are completely cooled, frost them with the almond frosting using a piping bag or a spatula.

Garnish:
- Garnish with sliced almonds on top of each cupcake.

Tips:

- Ensure that the butter and eggs are at room temperature for a smoother batter and frosting.
- If you prefer a more vibrant almond flavor, you can add a few drops of almond extract to the cupcake batter.

Enjoy these delightful Raspberry Almond Cupcakes with their almond-flavored frosting!

Carrot Cake Muffins

Ingredients:

For the Muffins:

- 1 1/2 cups all-purpose flour
- 1 teaspoon baking powder
- 1/2 teaspoon baking soda
- 1/2 teaspoon salt
- 1 teaspoon ground cinnamon
- 1/2 teaspoon ground nutmeg
- 1/4 teaspoon ground ginger
- 1/2 cup unsalted butter, melted
- 1/2 cup granulated sugar
- 1/2 cup packed brown sugar
- 2 large eggs
- 1 teaspoon vanilla extract
- 1 1/2 cups grated carrots (about 2-3 medium carrots)
- 1/2 cup crushed pineapple, drained
- 1/2 cup chopped walnuts or pecans (optional)

For the Cream Cheese Frosting:

- 8 ounces cream cheese, softened
- 1/4 cup unsalted butter, softened
- 2 cups powdered sugar
- 1 teaspoon vanilla extract

Instructions:

For the Muffins:

> Preheat the Oven:
> - Preheat your oven to 350°F (175°C). Line a muffin tin with paper liners.
>
> Mix Dry Ingredients:

- In a medium bowl, whisk together the flour, baking powder, baking soda, salt, cinnamon, nutmeg, and ginger. Set aside.

Combine Wet Ingredients:
- In a large mixing bowl, whisk together the melted butter, granulated sugar, brown sugar, eggs, and vanilla extract until well combined.

Add Dry Ingredients:
- Gradually add the dry ingredients to the wet ingredients, mixing until just combined.

Fold in Carrots, Pineapple, and Nuts:
- Gently fold in the grated carrots, crushed pineapple, and chopped nuts (if using) until evenly distributed throughout the batter.

Fill Muffin Cups:
- Divide the batter evenly among the muffin cups, filling each about 2/3 full.

Bake:
- Bake in the preheated oven for 20-25 minutes or until a toothpick inserted into the center of a muffin comes out clean.

Cool:
- Allow the carrot cake muffins to cool in the muffin tin for a few minutes, then transfer them to a wire rack to cool completely.

For the Cream Cheese Frosting:

Prepare Frosting:
- In a mixing bowl, beat the softened cream cheese and butter until smooth and creamy.

Add Powdered Sugar and Vanilla:
- Gradually add the powdered sugar, one cup at a time, and beat until well combined. Add the vanilla extract and continue to beat until fluffy.

Frost Muffins:
- Once the muffins are completely cooled, frost them with the cream cheese frosting using a piping bag or a spatula.

Optional: Garnish:
- Garnish with additional chopped nuts or a sprinkle of cinnamon if desired.

Tips:

- For a more moist texture, you can add 1/2 cup of crushed pineapple, well-drained, to the cream cheese frosting.

- Adjust the amount of nuts based on your preference or omit them for a nut-free version.

Enjoy these delicious Carrot Cake Muffins with the creamy goodness of cream cheese frosting!

Maple Pecan Muffins

Ingredients:

For the Muffins:

- 2 cups all-purpose flour
- 1 tablespoon baking powder
- 1/2 teaspoon baking soda
- 1/2 teaspoon salt
- 1 teaspoon ground cinnamon
- 1/2 cup unsalted butter, melted
- 1/2 cup granulated sugar
- 1/2 cup pure maple syrup
- 1 cup buttermilk
- 2 large eggs
- 1 teaspoon vanilla extract
- 1 cup chopped pecans

For the Maple Glaze:

- 1 cup powdered sugar
- 2 tablespoons pure maple syrup
- 1-2 tablespoons milk or cream
- Chopped pecans for garnish (optional)

Instructions:

For the Muffins:

Preheat the Oven:
- Preheat your oven to 375°F (190°C). Line a muffin tin with paper liners.

Mix Dry Ingredients:
- In a large bowl, whisk together the flour, baking powder, baking soda, salt, and ground cinnamon.

Combine Wet Ingredients:

- In another bowl, whisk together the melted butter, granulated sugar, maple syrup, buttermilk, eggs, and vanilla extract until well combined.

Add Wet Ingredients to Dry:
- Pour the wet ingredients into the dry ingredients and gently fold until just combined. Do not overmix.

Fold in Chopped Pecans:
- Gently fold in the chopped pecans until evenly distributed throughout the batter.

Fill Muffin Cups:
- Divide the batter evenly among the muffin cups, filling each about 2/3 full.

Bake:
- Bake in the preheated oven for 18-20 minutes or until a toothpick inserted into the center of a muffin comes out clean.

Cool:
- Allow the maple pecan muffins to cool in the muffin tin for a few minutes, then transfer them to a wire rack to cool completely.

For the Maple Glaze:

Prepare Glaze:
- In a small bowl, whisk together the powdered sugar, maple syrup, and milk or cream until smooth.

Glaze Muffins:
- Once the muffins are completely cooled, drizzle the maple glaze over the top. Garnish with additional chopped pecans if desired.

Tips:

- For an extra layer of flavor, you can add a pinch of nutmeg or a dash of maple extract to the batter.
- Ensure that the buttermilk, eggs, and butter are at room temperature for a smoother batter.

Enjoy these delightful Maple Pecan Muffins, perfect for a cozy breakfast or snack!

Double Chocolate Zucchini Muffins

Ingredients:

Dry Ingredients:

- 1 1/2 cups all-purpose flour
- 1/2 cup unsweetened cocoa powder
- 1 teaspoon baking powder
- 1/2 teaspoon baking soda
- 1/2 teaspoon salt

Wet Ingredients:

- 1/2 cup unsalted butter, melted
- 1/2 cup granulated sugar
- 1/2 cup brown sugar, packed
- 2 large eggs
- 1 teaspoon vanilla extract

Other Ingredients:

- 1 1/2 cups grated zucchini, squeezed and excess moisture removed
- 1/2 cup buttermilk
- 1 cup chocolate chips (semi-sweet or dark)

Instructions:

Preheat the Oven:
- Preheat your oven to 350°F (175°C). Line a muffin tin with paper liners.

Prepare Zucchini:
- Grate the zucchini and place it on a clean kitchen towel. Squeeze out excess moisture from the zucchini.

Mix Dry Ingredients:
- In a large bowl, whisk together the flour, cocoa powder, baking powder, baking soda, and salt.

Combine Wet Ingredients:

- In another bowl, whisk together the melted butter, granulated sugar, brown sugar, eggs, and vanilla extract until well combined.

Add Grated Zucchini:
- Stir the grated zucchini into the wet ingredients.

Alternate Wet and Dry Ingredients:
- Gradually add the dry ingredients to the wet ingredients, alternating with the buttermilk. Begin and end with the dry ingredients. Mix until just combined.

Fold in Chocolate Chips:
- Gently fold in the chocolate chips until evenly distributed throughout the batter.

Fill Muffin Cups:
- Divide the batter evenly among the muffin cups, filling each about 2/3 full.

Bake:
- Bake in the preheated oven for 18-20 minutes or until a toothpick inserted into the center of a muffin comes out clean.

Cool:
- Allow the double chocolate zucchini muffins to cool in the muffin tin for a few minutes, then transfer them to a wire rack to cool completely.

Tips:

- You can add a handful of chopped nuts (such as walnuts or pecans) for added texture.
- For an extra moist texture, you can substitute part of the butter with vegetable oil.

Enjoy these moist and chocolatey Double Chocolate Zucchini Muffins – a delicious way to sneak in some veggies!

Orange Cranberry Muffins

Ingredients:

Dry Ingredients:

- 2 cups all-purpose flour
- 1 cup granulated sugar
- 1 1/2 teaspoons baking powder
- 1/2 teaspoon baking soda
- 1/4 teaspoon salt

Wet Ingredients:

- 1/2 cup unsalted butter, melted
- 3/4 cup freshly squeezed orange juice
- Zest of 1 orange
- 2 large eggs
- 1 teaspoon vanilla extract

Other Ingredients:

- 1 1/2 cups fresh or frozen cranberries, coarsely chopped

For the Glaze:

- 1 cup powdered sugar
- 2 tablespoons freshly squeezed orange juice
- Zest of 1 orange (optional)

Instructions:

Preheat the Oven:
- Preheat your oven to 375°F (190°C). Line a muffin tin with paper liners.

Mix Dry Ingredients:
- In a large bowl, whisk together the flour, sugar, baking powder, baking soda, and salt.

Combine Wet Ingredients:
- In another bowl, whisk together the melted butter, orange juice, orange zest, eggs, and vanilla extract until well combined.

Combine Wet and Dry Ingredients:
- Gradually add the wet ingredients to the dry ingredients, stirring until just combined. Do not overmix.

Fold in Cranberries:
- Gently fold in the chopped cranberries until evenly distributed throughout the batter.

Fill Muffin Cups:
- Divide the batter evenly among the muffin cups, filling each about 2/3 full.

Bake:
- Bake in the preheated oven for 18-20 minutes or until a toothpick inserted into the center of a muffin comes out clean.

Cool:
- Allow the orange cranberry muffins to cool in the muffin tin for a few minutes, then transfer them to a wire rack to cool completely.

For the Glaze:

Prepare Glaze:
- In a small bowl, whisk together the powdered sugar and orange juice until smooth.

Glaze Muffins:
- Once the muffins are completely cooled, drizzle the orange glaze over the top. Sprinkle with additional orange zest if desired.

Tips:

- You can use dried cranberries if fresh or frozen cranberries are not available.
- For an extra burst of flavor, add a pinch of ground cinnamon or nutmeg to the dry ingredients.

Enjoy these bright and flavorful Orange Cranberry Muffins with a zesty orange glaze!

Snickerdoodle Cupcakes

Ingredients:

For the Cupcakes:

- 1 1/2 cups all-purpose flour
- 1 1/2 teaspoons baking powder
- 1/2 teaspoon baking soda
- 1/2 teaspoon salt
- 1/2 cup unsalted butter, softened
- 1 cup granulated sugar
- 2 large eggs
- 1 teaspoon vanilla extract
- 1/2 cup sour cream
- 1/2 cup whole milk

For the Cinnamon Sugar Topping:

- 1/4 cup granulated sugar
- 1 teaspoon ground cinnamon

For the Cinnamon Cream Cheese Frosting:

- 8 ounces cream cheese, softened
- 1/2 cup unsalted butter, softened
- 4 cups powdered sugar
- 1 teaspoon ground cinnamon
- 1 teaspoon vanilla extract

Instructions:

For the Cupcakes:

   Preheat the Oven:
   - Preheat your oven to 350°F (175°C). Line a muffin tin with paper liners.

   Mix Dry Ingredients:

- In a medium bowl, whisk together the flour, baking powder, baking soda, and salt. Set aside.

Cream Butter and Sugar:
- In a large mixing bowl, cream together the softened butter and granulated sugar until light and fluffy.

Add Eggs and Vanilla:
- Beat in the eggs one at a time, then mix in the vanilla extract.

Alternate Wet and Dry Ingredients:
- Gradually add the dry ingredients to the wet ingredients, alternating with the sour cream and milk. Begin and end with the dry ingredients. Mix until just combined.

Fill Cupcake Liners:
- Divide the batter evenly among the muffin cups, filling each about 2/3 full.

Cinnamon Sugar Topping:
- In a small bowl, combine the granulated sugar and ground cinnamon. Sprinkle the cinnamon sugar mixture over the top of each cupcake batter.

Bake:
- Bake in the preheated oven for 18-20 minutes or until a toothpick inserted into the center of a cupcake comes out clean.

Cool:
- Allow the snickerdoodle cupcakes to cool in the muffin tin for a few minutes, then transfer them to a wire rack to cool completely.

For the Cinnamon Cream Cheese Frosting:

Prepare Frosting:
- In a mixing bowl, beat the softened cream cheese and butter until smooth and creamy.

Add Powdered Sugar, Cinnamon, and Vanilla:
- Gradually add the powdered sugar, ground cinnamon, and vanilla extract. Beat until well combined and fluffy.

Frost Cupcakes:
- Once the cupcakes are completely cooled, frost them with the cinnamon cream cheese frosting using a piping bag or a spatula.

Optional: Garnish:
- Garnish with an additional sprinkle of cinnamon or a cinnamon stick if desired.

Tips:

- For an extra touch, you can roll the tops of the cupcakes in cinnamon sugar before frosting.
- Adjust the level of cinnamon in the frosting to suit your taste.

Enjoy these delightful and cinnamon-sugar-kissed Snickerdoodle Cupcakes!

Breads and Rolls:
Chocolate Chip Cookies

Ingredients:

- 1 cup (2 sticks) unsalted butter, softened
- 3/4 cup granulated sugar
- 3/4 cup packed brown sugar
- 2 large eggs
- 1 teaspoon vanilla extract
- 2 1/4 cups all-purpose flour
- 1 teaspoon baking soda
- 1/2 teaspoon salt
- 2 cups semisweet chocolate chips
- 1 cup chopped nuts (optional)

Instructions:

Preheat the Oven:
- Preheat your oven to 375°F (190°C). Line baking sheets with parchment paper.

Cream Butter and Sugars:
- In a large mixing bowl, cream together the softened butter, granulated sugar, and brown sugar until light and fluffy.

Add Eggs and Vanilla:
- Beat in the eggs one at a time, then mix in the vanilla extract.

Combine Dry Ingredients:
- In a separate bowl, whisk together the flour, baking soda, and salt.

Add Dry Ingredients to Wet Ingredients:
- Gradually add the dry ingredients to the wet ingredients, mixing until just combined.

Fold in Chocolate Chips and Nuts:
- Gently fold in the chocolate chips and nuts (if using) until evenly distributed throughout the dough.

Drop Dough onto Baking Sheets:
- Drop rounded tablespoons of dough onto the prepared baking sheets, spacing them about 2 inches apart.

Bake:

- Bake in the preheated oven for 9-11 minutes or until the edges are golden but the centers are still soft.

Cool:
- Allow the cookies to cool on the baking sheets for a few minutes before transferring them to wire racks to cool completely.

Tips:

- If you prefer a chewier cookie, slightly underbake them and let them finish setting up on the baking sheets outside the oven.
- For an extra flavor boost, add a pinch of sea salt to the tops of the cookies before baking.

Enjoy these classic and delicious Chocolate Chip Cookies!

Oatmeal Raisin Cookies

Ingredients:

- 1 cup (2 sticks) unsalted butter, softened
- 1 cup packed brown sugar
- 1/2 cup granulated sugar
- 2 large eggs
- 1 teaspoon vanilla extract
- 1 1/2 cups all-purpose flour
- 1 teaspoon baking soda
- 1 teaspoon ground cinnamon
- 1/2 teaspoon salt
- 3 cups old-fashioned oats
- 1 cup raisins

Instructions:

Preheat the Oven:
- Preheat your oven to 350°F (175°C). Line baking sheets with parchment paper.

Cream Butter and Sugars:
- In a large mixing bowl, cream together the softened butter, packed brown sugar, and granulated sugar until light and fluffy.

Add Eggs and Vanilla:
- Beat in the eggs one at a time, then mix in the vanilla extract.

Combine Dry Ingredients:
- In a separate bowl, whisk together the flour, baking soda, ground cinnamon, and salt.

Add Dry Ingredients to Wet Ingredients:
- Gradually add the dry ingredients to the wet ingredients, mixing until just combined.

Fold in Oats and Raisins:
- Gently fold in the old-fashioned oats and raisins until evenly distributed throughout the dough.

Drop Dough onto Baking Sheets:
- Drop rounded tablespoons of dough onto the prepared baking sheets, spacing them about 2 inches apart.

Bake:

- Bake in the preheated oven for 10-12 minutes or until the edges are golden but the centers are still soft.

Cool:
- Allow the oatmeal raisin cookies to cool on the baking sheets for a few minutes before transferring them to wire racks to cool completely.

Tips:

- You can soak the raisins in hot water for about 10 minutes, then drain them before adding to the cookie dough. This helps to plump them up.
- For added texture, consider adding chopped nuts (such as walnuts or pecans) to the cookie dough.

Enjoy these hearty and chewy Oatmeal Raisin Cookies!

Peanut Butter Blossoms

Ingredients:

- 1/2 cup (1 stick) unsalted butter, softened
- 1/2 cup granulated sugar
- 1/2 cup packed brown sugar
- 1/2 cup creamy peanut butter
- 1 large egg
- 1 teaspoon vanilla extract
- 1 3/4 cups all-purpose flour
- 1 teaspoon baking soda
- 1/2 teaspoon salt
- Additional granulated sugar for rolling
- 36 chocolate Hershey's Kisses, unwrapped

Instructions:

Preheat the Oven:
- Preheat your oven to 375°F (190°C). Line baking sheets with parchment paper.

Cream Butter and Sugars:
- In a large mixing bowl, cream together the softened butter, granulated sugar, brown sugar, and peanut butter until light and fluffy.

Add Egg and Vanilla:
- Beat in the egg and vanilla extract until well combined.

Combine Dry Ingredients:
- In a separate bowl, whisk together the flour, baking soda, and salt.

Add Dry Ingredients to Wet Ingredients:
- Gradually add the dry ingredients to the wet ingredients, mixing until just combined.

Shape Dough into Balls:
- Shape the dough into 1-inch balls. Roll each ball in additional granulated sugar to coat.

Bake:
- Place the coated dough balls on the prepared baking sheets, spacing them about 2 inches apart. Bake in the preheated oven for 8-10 minutes or until the edges are golden.

Add Hershey's Kisses:
- Remove the cookies from the oven and immediately press a Hershey's Kiss into the center of each cookie. The edges may crack slightly.

Cool:
- Allow the peanut butter blossoms to cool on the baking sheets for a few minutes before transferring them to wire racks to cool completely.

Tips:

- If you prefer a softer cookie, reduce the baking time to 8 minutes.
- Experiment with different Hershey's Kiss flavors, such as dark chocolate or caramel-filled, for variety.

Enjoy these classic and irresistible Peanut Butter Blossoms!

White Chocolate Macadamia Nut Cookies

Ingredients:

- 1 cup (2 sticks) unsalted butter, softened
- 1 cup granulated sugar
- 1 cup packed brown sugar
- 2 large eggs
- 1 teaspoon vanilla extract
- 3 cups all-purpose flour
- 1 teaspoon baking soda
- 1/2 teaspoon baking powder
- 1/2 teaspoon salt
- 1 1/2 cups white chocolate chips
- 1 cup macadamia nuts, chopped

Instructions:

Preheat the Oven:
- Preheat your oven to 350°F (175°C). Line baking sheets with parchment paper.

Cream Butter and Sugars:
- In a large mixing bowl, cream together the softened butter, granulated sugar, and brown sugar until light and fluffy.

Add Eggs and Vanilla:
- Beat in the eggs one at a time, then mix in the vanilla extract.

Combine Dry Ingredients:
- In a separate bowl, whisk together the flour, baking soda, baking powder, and salt.

Add Dry Ingredients to Wet Ingredients:
- Gradually add the dry ingredients to the wet ingredients, mixing until just combined.

Fold in White Chocolate Chips and Macadamia Nuts:
- Gently fold in the white chocolate chips and chopped macadamia nuts until evenly distributed throughout the dough.

Shape Dough into Balls:
- Drop rounded tablespoons of dough onto the prepared baking sheets, spacing them about 2 inches apart.

Bake:
- Bake in the preheated oven for 10-12 minutes or until the edges are golden.

Cool:
- Allow the white chocolate macadamia nut cookies to cool on the baking sheets for a few minutes before transferring them to wire racks to cool completely.

Tips:

- If you want a slightly chewier texture, slightly underbake the cookies and allow them to finish setting up on the baking sheets.
- Toasting the macadamia nuts before adding them to the cookie dough enhances their flavor. Simply bake them in a preheated oven at 350°F (175°C) for 5-7 minutes, or until golden.

Enjoy these rich and indulgent White Chocolate Macadamia Nut Cookies!

Double Chocolate Mint Cookies

Ingredients:

- 1 cup (2 sticks) unsalted butter, softened
- 1 cup granulated sugar
- 3/4 cup packed brown sugar
- 2 large eggs
- 1 teaspoon vanilla extract
- 2 cups all-purpose flour
- 1/2 cup unsweetened cocoa powder
- 1 teaspoon baking soda
- 1/4 teaspoon salt
- 1 cup dark or semi-sweet chocolate chips
- 1 cup mint chocolate chips or chopped mint chocolate
- Optional: Crushed candy canes for topping

Instructions:

Preheat the Oven:
- Preheat your oven to 350°F (175°C). Line baking sheets with parchment paper.

Cream Butter and Sugars:
- In a large mixing bowl, cream together the softened butter, granulated sugar, and brown sugar until light and fluffy.

Add Eggs and Vanilla:
- Beat in the eggs one at a time, then mix in the vanilla extract.

Combine Dry Ingredients:
- In a separate bowl, whisk together the flour, cocoa powder, baking soda, and salt.

Add Dry Ingredients to Wet Ingredients:
- Gradually add the dry ingredients to the wet ingredients, mixing until just combined.

Fold in Chocolate Chips:
- Gently fold in the dark or semi-sweet chocolate chips and mint chocolate chips until evenly distributed throughout the dough.

Shape Dough into Balls:

- Drop rounded tablespoons of dough onto the prepared baking sheets, spacing them about 2 inches apart.

Bake:
- Bake in the preheated oven for 10-12 minutes or until the edges are set. The centers may still be soft.

Optional: Top with Crushed Candy Canes:
- If desired, immediately after removing the cookies from the oven, press a few pieces of crushed candy canes onto the tops of the cookies.

Cool:
- Allow the double chocolate mint cookies to cool on the baking sheets for a few minutes before transferring them to wire racks to cool completely.

Tips:

- For an extra minty flavor, consider adding 1/2 teaspoon of peppermint extract to the cookie dough.
- If you can't find mint chocolate chips, you can use regular chocolate chips and add 1/2 teaspoon of peppermint extract to the dough.

Enjoy these decadent and minty Double Chocolate Mint Cookies!

Almond Butter Cookies

Ingredients:

- 1 cup almond butter (unsweetened)
- 1/2 cup unsalted butter, softened
- 1 cup granulated sugar
- 1 cup packed brown sugar
- 2 large eggs
- 1 teaspoon vanilla extract
- 2 1/2 cups all-purpose flour
- 1/2 teaspoon baking soda
- 1/2 teaspoon baking powder
- 1/4 teaspoon salt
- Sliced almonds for garnish (optional)

Instructions:

Preheat the Oven:
- Preheat your oven to 350°F (175°C). Line baking sheets with parchment paper.

Cream Almond Butter, Butter, and Sugars:
- In a large mixing bowl, cream together the almond butter, softened butter, granulated sugar, and brown sugar until light and fluffy.

Add Eggs and Vanilla:
- Beat in the eggs one at a time, then mix in the vanilla extract.

Combine Dry Ingredients:
- In a separate bowl, whisk together the flour, baking soda, baking powder, and salt.

Add Dry Ingredients to Wet Ingredients:
- Gradually add the dry ingredients to the wet ingredients, mixing until just combined.

Shape Dough into Balls:
- Drop rounded tablespoons of dough onto the prepared baking sheets, spacing them about 2 inches apart.

Optional: Garnish with Sliced Almonds:
- If desired, press a few sliced almonds onto the tops of the cookie dough balls for garnish.

Bake:

- Bake in the preheated oven for 10-12 minutes or until the edges are golden. The centers may still be slightly soft.

Cool:
- Allow the almond butter cookies to cool on the baking sheets for a few minutes before transferring them to wire racks to cool completely.

Tips:

- If your almond butter is unsalted, you may want to add a pinch of salt to the cookie dough for balance.
- For a nuttier flavor, you can use roasted almond butter.

Enjoy these delicious and nutty Almond Butter Cookies!

Lemon Shortbread Cookies

Ingredients:

- 1 cup unsalted butter, softened
- 1/2 cup powdered sugar
- 2 cups all-purpose flour
- Zest of 2 lemons
- 2 tablespoons fresh lemon juice
- 1/4 teaspoon salt
- Additional powdered sugar for dusting (optional)

Instructions:

Preheat the Oven:
- Preheat your oven to 350°F (175°C). Line baking sheets with parchment paper.

Cream Butter and Powdered Sugar:
- In a large mixing bowl, cream together the softened butter and powdered sugar until light and fluffy.

Add Lemon Zest and Juice:
- Mix in the lemon zest and fresh lemon juice until well combined.

Combine Dry Ingredients:
- In a separate bowl, whisk together the flour and salt.

Add Dry Ingredients to Wet Ingredients:
- Gradually add the dry ingredients to the wet ingredients, mixing until just combined. Do not overmix.

Shape Dough:
- Form the dough into a ball and wrap it in plastic wrap. Chill in the refrigerator for at least 30 minutes.

Roll and Cut Cookies:
- On a lightly floured surface, roll out the chilled dough to a thickness of about 1/4 inch. Use cookie cutters to cut out shapes and place them on the prepared baking sheets.

Bake:
- Bake in the preheated oven for 10-12 minutes or until the edges are just beginning to turn golden. The cookies will continue to firm up as they cool.

Cool:

- Allow the lemon shortbread cookies to cool on the baking sheets for a few minutes before transferring them to wire racks to cool completely.

Optional: Dust with Powdered Sugar:
- If desired, dust the cooled cookies with additional powdered sugar before serving.

Tips:

- For a more intense lemon flavor, you can add a few drops of lemon extract to the dough.
- These cookies can be stored in an airtight container for several days, and their flavor often improves over time.

Enjoy these delicate and citrusy Lemon Shortbread Cookies!

Coconut Macaroons

Ingredients:

- 3 cups sweetened shredded coconut
- 3/4 cup sweetened condensed milk
- 1 teaspoon vanilla extract
- 2 large egg whites
- 1/4 teaspoon salt
- Optional: 1 cup chocolate chips (for dipping)

Instructions:

Preheat the Oven:
- Preheat your oven to 325°F (160°C). Line baking sheets with parchment paper.

Mix Coconut, Sweetened Condensed Milk, and Vanilla:
- In a large bowl, combine the shredded coconut, sweetened condensed milk, and vanilla extract. Mix well until evenly combined.

Whip Egg Whites with Salt:
- In a separate bowl, whip the egg whites and salt until stiff peaks form.

Fold Egg Whites into Coconut Mixture:
- Gently fold the whipped egg whites into the coconut mixture until well combined. Be careful not to deflate the egg whites.

Shape Macaroons:
- Using a spoon or cookie scoop, drop rounded mounds of the coconut mixture onto the prepared baking sheets. Space them about 2 inches apart.

Bake:
- Bake in the preheated oven for 15-20 minutes or until the edges of the macaroons are golden brown.

Optional: Dip in Chocolate:
- If desired, melt chocolate chips in a microwave or on the stovetop. Dip the bottoms of the cooled macaroons into the melted chocolate and place them on parchment paper to set.

Cool:
- Allow the coconut macaroons to cool on the baking sheets for a few minutes before transferring them to wire racks to cool completely.

Tips:

- Ensure that the egg whites are free from any traces of egg yolk, as even a small amount of yolk can prevent the whites from reaching stiff peaks.
- For an extra touch, you can add a pinch of almond extract to the coconut mixture for a hint of almond flavor.

Enjoy these sweet and chewy Coconut Macaroons!

Espresso Chocolate Chunk Cookies

Ingredients:

- 1 cup unsalted butter, softened
- 1 cup granulated sugar
- 1 cup brown sugar, packed
- 2 large eggs
- 2 teaspoons vanilla extract
- 2 tablespoons instant espresso powder
- 3 cups all-purpose flour
- 1 teaspoon baking soda
- 1/2 teaspoon salt
- 8 ounces dark chocolate, coarsely chopped
- Optional: 1 cup chopped nuts (such as walnuts or pecans)

Instructions:

Preheat the Oven:
- Preheat your oven to 350°F (175°C). Line baking sheets with parchment paper.

Dissolve Espresso Powder:
- In a small bowl, dissolve the instant espresso powder in 1 tablespoon of hot water. Set aside to cool.

Cream Butter and Sugars:
- In a large mixing bowl, cream together the softened butter, granulated sugar, and brown sugar until light and fluffy.

Add Eggs, Vanilla, and Espresso:
- Beat in the eggs one at a time, then mix in the vanilla extract and the dissolved espresso.

Combine Dry Ingredients:
- In a separate bowl, whisk together the flour, baking soda, and salt.

Add Dry Ingredients to Wet Ingredients:
- Gradually add the dry ingredients to the wet ingredients, mixing until just combined.

Fold in Chocolate Chunks and Nuts:
- Gently fold in the coarsely chopped dark chocolate and chopped nuts (if using) until evenly distributed throughout the dough.

Shape Dough into Balls:

- Drop rounded tablespoons of dough onto the prepared baking sheets, spacing them about 2 inches apart.

Bake:
- Bake in the preheated oven for 10-12 minutes or until the edges are golden. The centers may still be slightly soft.

Cool:
- Allow the espresso chocolate chunk cookies to cool on the baking sheets for a few minutes before transferring them to wire racks to cool completely.

Tips:

- If you prefer a more pronounced espresso flavor, you can add an extra teaspoon of instant espresso powder.
- Using high-quality dark chocolate with at least 60% cocoa content enhances the richness of these cookies.

Enjoy these Espresso Chocolate Chunk Cookies, perfect for coffee and chocolate lovers alike!

Pistachio Cranberry Biscotti

Ingredients:

- 2 cups all-purpose flour
- 1 cup granulated sugar
- 1 teaspoon baking powder
- 1/2 teaspoon salt
- 3 large eggs
- 1 teaspoon vanilla extract
- 1 cup shelled pistachios, chopped
- 1 cup dried cranberries

For the Optional Chocolate Drizzle:

- 1/2 cup white or dark chocolate chips
- 1 teaspoon vegetable oil

Instructions:

Preheat the Oven:
- Preheat your oven to 350°F (175°C). Line a baking sheet with parchment paper.

Mix Dry Ingredients:
- In a large bowl, whisk together the flour, sugar, baking powder, and salt.

Combine Wet Ingredients:
- In a separate bowl, beat the eggs and vanilla extract until well combined.

Combine Wet and Dry Ingredients:
- Add the wet ingredients to the dry ingredients, stirring until just combined.

Fold in Pistachios and Cranberries:
- Gently fold in the chopped pistachios and dried cranberries until evenly distributed throughout the dough.

Shape Dough:
- Divide the dough in half. On a floured surface, shape each half into a log about 12 inches long and 2 inches wide.

Bake:
- Place the logs on the prepared baking sheet and bake in the preheated oven for 25-30 minutes or until firm and golden.

Cool:

- Allow the biscotti logs to cool on the baking sheet for about 10 minutes.

Slice Biscotti:
- Using a sharp knife, slice the logs diagonally into 1/2-inch thick slices.

Bake Again:
- Place the sliced biscotti back on the baking sheet, cut sides down, and bake for an additional 10-15 minutes or until they are crisp and golden.

Optional Chocolate Drizzle:
- If desired, melt the chocolate chips with vegetable oil in a microwave or on the stovetop. Drizzle the melted chocolate over the cooled biscotti.

Cool Completely:
- Allow the biscotti to cool completely before serving or storing.

Tips:

- You can customize the biscotti by adding a teaspoon of orange zest or almond extract for extra flavor.
- To enhance the chocolate drizzle, consider adding a sprinkle of finely chopped pistachios on top.

Enjoy these delightful Pistachio Cranberry Biscotti with your favorite hot beverage!

Pastries and Tarts:

Apple Turnovers

Ingredients:

For the Filling:

- 3 cups peeled, cored, and diced apples (such as Granny Smith)
- 1/2 cup granulated sugar
- 1 teaspoon ground cinnamon
- 1/4 teaspoon nutmeg
- 2 tablespoons all-purpose flour
- 1 tablespoon lemon juice

For the Pastry:

- 2 sheets puff pastry, thawed if frozen
- 1 egg (for egg wash)
- 1 tablespoon water (for egg wash)
- Powdered sugar for dusting (optional)

Instructions:

Preheat the Oven:
- Preheat your oven to 375°F (190°C). Line a baking sheet with parchment paper.

Prepare the Filling:
- In a mixing bowl, combine the diced apples, granulated sugar, ground cinnamon, nutmeg, all-purpose flour, and lemon juice. Toss until the apples are evenly coated. Set aside.

Roll Out the Puff Pastry:
- On a lightly floured surface, roll out each sheet of puff pastry to approximately 10x10 inches.

Cut into Squares:
- Cut each sheet into four squares.

Fill and Seal:

- Place a spoonful of the apple filling in the center of each pastry square. Fold the pastry over to create a triangle, enclosing the filling. Press the edges to seal. You can use a fork to crimp the edges.

Make Egg Wash:
- In a small bowl, whisk together the egg and water to create an egg wash.

Brush with Egg Wash:
- Brush the tops of the turnovers with the egg wash. This will give them a golden-brown color when baked.

Ventilation:
- Use a sharp knife to make a few small slits on the top of each turnover to allow steam to escape during baking.

Bake:
- Place the turnovers on the prepared baking sheet and bake in the preheated oven for 20-25 minutes or until they are golden brown and puffed.

Cool:
- Allow the apple turnovers to cool slightly on the baking sheet before transferring them to a wire rack to cool completely.

Optional: Dust with Powdered Sugar:
- If desired, dust the cooled turnovers with powdered sugar before serving.

Tips:

- Serve the turnovers warm for the best flavor. They can be enjoyed on their own or with a scoop of vanilla ice cream.
- Feel free to add raisins or chopped nuts to the filling for extra texture.

Enjoy these delicious homemade Apple Turnovers!

Strawberry Danish

Ingredients:

For the Dough:

- 2 1/4 teaspoons (1 packet) active dry yeast
- 1/4 cup warm water (about 110°F or 43°C)
- 1/2 cup milk, warmed
- 1/4 cup granulated sugar
- 1/2 cup unsalted butter, softened
- 1/2 teaspoon salt
- 2 1/2 cups all-purpose flour
- 1 large egg

For the Strawberry Filling:

- 1 1/2 cups fresh strawberries, hulled and sliced
- 1/4 cup granulated sugar
- 1 tablespoon cornstarch
- 1 teaspoon vanilla extract
- Zest of one lemon (optional)

For the Cream Cheese Filling:

- 4 ounces cream cheese, softened
- 1/4 cup powdered sugar
- 1/2 teaspoon vanilla extract

For the Glaze:

- 1/2 cup powdered sugar
- 1-2 tablespoons milk
- 1/2 teaspoon vanilla extract

Instructions:

Prepare the Dough:

- Activate Yeast:
  - In a small bowl, dissolve the yeast in warm water. Let it sit for about 5 minutes until frothy.
- Combine Ingredients:
  - In a large mixing bowl, combine the warm milk, granulated sugar, softened butter, salt, and half of the flour. Add the activated yeast and mix well.
- Add Egg and Flour:
  - Beat in the egg. Gradually add the remaining flour until a soft dough forms.
- Knead Dough:
  - Turn the dough onto a floured surface and knead for about 5-7 minutes until smooth and elastic.
- First Rise:
  - Place the dough in a greased bowl, cover with a kitchen towel, and let it rise in a warm place for 1-2 hours or until doubled in size.

Prepare the Strawberry Filling:

- Mix Ingredients:
  - In a medium bowl, toss together the sliced strawberries, granulated sugar, cornstarch, vanilla extract, and lemon zest (if using). Set aside.

Prepare the Cream Cheese Filling:

- Combine Ingredients:
  - In a small bowl, mix together the softened cream cheese, powdered sugar, and vanilla extract until smooth. Set aside.

Assemble and Bake:

- Preheat Oven:
  - Preheat your oven to 375°F (190°C). Line a baking sheet with parchment paper.
- Roll Out Dough:
  - On a floured surface, roll out the risen dough into a large rectangle.
- Add Fillings:

- Spread the cream cheese filling down the center of the dough. Top it with the strawberry filling.

Cut and Twist:
- Cut 1-inch wide strips on either side of the filling. Twist each strip and place it over the filling, creating a braided appearance.

Second Rise:
- Allow the assembled Danish to rise for an additional 15-20 minutes.

Bake:
- Bake in the preheated oven for 20-25 minutes or until golden brown.

Prepare the Glaze:

Mix Ingredients:
- In a small bowl, whisk together the powdered sugar, milk, and vanilla extract to make the glaze.

Glaze Danish:
- Drizzle the glaze over the warm Danish as soon as it comes out of the oven.

Cool:
- Allow the Strawberry Danish to cool slightly before slicing and serving.

Tips:

- You can customize the filling by using other fruits such as blueberries, raspberries, or a combination.
- Serve the Danish warm for the best flavor.

Enjoy your homemade Strawberry Danish!

Chocolate Croissants (Pain au Chocolat)

Ingredients:

For the Dough:

- 1 1/4 cups warm milk (about 110°F or 43°C)
- 2 teaspoons active dry yeast
- 1/4 cup granulated sugar
- 3 1/2 cups all-purpose flour
- 1 teaspoon salt
- 1 cup unsalted butter, cold

For the Filling:

- 8 ounces dark chocolate, chopped (or chocolate chips)
- 1/4 cup powdered sugar (optional)

For Egg Wash:

- 1 large egg
- 1 tablespoon water

Instructions:

Prepare the Dough:

    Activate Yeast:
- In a small bowl, combine warm milk, yeast, and a pinch of sugar. Let it sit for about 5 minutes until frothy.

    Combine Dry Ingredients:
- In a large bowl, whisk together the remaining sugar, flour, and salt.

    Mix Dough:
- Pour the activated yeast mixture into the flour mixture and knead until a soft dough forms.

    Chill Dough:
- Wrap the dough in plastic wrap and refrigerate for 1 hour.

Prepare Butter Block:
- Place the cold butter between two sheets of parchment paper. Roll it out into a 1/2-inch thick rectangle.

Enclose Butter in Dough:
- Roll out the chilled dough on a floured surface into a larger rectangle. Place the butter block in the center and fold the dough over it, sealing the edges.

Fold and Chill:
- Roll out the dough again, fold it into thirds like a letter, and refrigerate for 30 minutes. Repeat this process two more times.

Shape and Fill the Croissants:

Roll Out Dough:
- Roll out the chilled dough into a large rectangle.

Cut and Fill:
- Cut the dough into rectangles. Place chopped chocolate or chocolate chips at one end of each rectangle. Optionally, sprinkle with powdered sugar.

Roll Up:
- Roll the dough from the chocolate end towards the other end, enclosing the chocolate.

Egg Wash:
- Whisk together the egg and water to make an egg wash. Brush the tops of the croissants with the egg wash.

Proofing:
- Place the shaped croissants on a baking sheet and let them proof for about 1-2 hours or until doubled in size.

Bake:

Preheat Oven:
- Preheat your oven to 400°F (200°C).

Egg Wash Again:
- Before baking, brush the croissants with another layer of egg wash.

Bake:
- Bake in the preheated oven for 15-20 minutes or until the croissants are golden brown and flaky.

Cool:
- Allow the chocolate croissants to cool on a wire rack before serving.

Tips:

- You can make these ahead of time and freeze them before baking. When ready to bake, let them thaw and rise, then proceed with the baking instructions.
- Experiment with different types of chocolate for the filling, such as milk chocolate or white chocolate.

Enjoy your delicious homemade Chocolate Croissants!

Mixed Berry Galette

Ingredients:

For the Dough:

- 1 1/4 cups all-purpose flour
- 1 tablespoon granulated sugar
- 1/4 teaspoon salt
- 1/2 cup unsalted butter, cold and cut into small cubes
- 3-4 tablespoons ice water

For the Filling:

- 2 cups mixed berries (such as strawberries, blueberries, raspberries, and blackberries)
- 1/4 cup granulated sugar
- 2 tablespoons cornstarch
- 1 tablespoon lemon juice
- 1 teaspoon vanilla extract

For Assembly:

- 1 tablespoon milk (for brushing the edges)
- 1 tablespoon turbinado sugar (for sprinkling)

Instructions:

Prepare the Dough:

>Combine Dry Ingredients:
>- In a food processor, pulse together the flour, sugar, and salt.
>
>Add Butter:
>- Add the cold butter cubes to the flour mixture and pulse until the mixture resembles coarse crumbs.
>
>Add Ice Water:

- Drizzle in the ice water, one tablespoon at a time, and pulse until the dough just comes together.

Form Dough:
- Turn the dough out onto a floured surface, shape it into a disc, wrap in plastic wrap, and refrigerate for at least 30 minutes.

Prepare the Filling:

Mix Berries and Ingredients:
- In a bowl, gently toss together the mixed berries, granulated sugar, cornstarch, lemon juice, and vanilla extract. Set aside.

Assemble the Galette:

Preheat Oven:
- Preheat your oven to 400°F (200°C). Line a baking sheet with parchment paper.

Roll Out Dough:
- On a floured surface, roll out the chilled dough into a circle about 12 inches in diameter.

Transfer to Baking Sheet:
- Carefully transfer the rolled-out dough to the prepared baking sheet.

Add Filling:
- Spoon the mixed berry filling onto the center of the dough, leaving a border around the edges.

Fold Edges:
- Fold the edges of the dough over the filling, pleating as you go to create a rustic edge.

Brush with Milk and Sprinkle with Sugar:
- Brush the edges of the galette with milk and sprinkle turbinado sugar over the crust for a golden finish.

Bake:
- Bake in the preheated oven for 25-30 minutes or until the crust is golden and the filling is bubbly.

Cool:
- Allow the mixed berry galette to cool on the baking sheet for a few minutes before transferring it to a wire rack to cool completely.

Serve:

- Serve the mixed berry galette warm or at room temperature. Optionally, dust with powdered sugar or serve with a scoop of vanilla ice cream.

Tips:

- Feel free to adjust the amount of sugar in the filling based on the sweetness of your berries.
- You can experiment with different combinations of berries to suit your taste.

Enjoy this simple and delicious Mixed Berry Galette!

Lemon Tart

Ingredients:

For the Tart Crust:

- 1 1/2 cups all-purpose flour
- 1/2 cup powdered sugar
- 1/4 teaspoon salt
- 1/2 cup unsalted butter, cold and cut into small cubes
- 1 large egg yolk
- 1-2 tablespoons ice water

For the Lemon Filling:

- 4 large eggs
- 1 cup granulated sugar
- 1 cup fresh lemon juice (about 4-6 lemons)
- Zest of 2 lemons
- 1/2 cup unsalted butter, melted

For Assembly:

- Powdered sugar for dusting
- Fresh berries for garnish (optional)

Instructions:

Prepare the Tart Crust:

> Combine Dry Ingredients:
> - In a food processor, pulse together the flour, powdered sugar, and salt.
>
> Add Butter:
> - Add the cold butter cubes to the flour mixture and pulse until the mixture resembles coarse crumbs.
>
> Add Egg Yolk and Ice Water:

- Add the egg yolk and pulse. Gradually add ice water, one tablespoon at a time, and pulse until the dough comes together.

Form Dough:
- Turn the dough out onto a floured surface, shape it into a disc, wrap in plastic wrap, and refrigerate for at least 30 minutes.

Preheat Oven and Roll Out Dough:

Preheat Oven:
- Preheat your oven to 375°F (190°C).

Roll Out Dough:
- On a floured surface, roll out the chilled dough to fit a 9-inch tart pan. Press the dough into the pan, trimming any excess.

Poke Holes and Chill:
- Use a fork to poke holes in the bottom of the crust. Chill the crust in the refrigerator for 15 minutes.

Blind Bake:
- Line the chilled crust with parchment paper and fill it with pie weights or dried beans. Bake for 15 minutes. Remove the weights and parchment, then bake for an additional 5-7 minutes or until the crust is golden. Allow it to cool while preparing the filling.

Prepare the Lemon Filling:

Whisk Eggs and Sugar:
- In a bowl, whisk together the eggs and granulated sugar until well combined.

Add Lemon Juice and Zest:
- Add the fresh lemon juice and lemon zest to the egg mixture, whisking until smooth.

Add Melted Butter:
- Pour in the melted butter and whisk until the filling is well combined.

Bake the Tart:

Pour Filling into Crust:
- Pour the lemon filling into the pre-baked tart crust.

Bake:

- Bake in the preheated oven for 20-25 minutes or until the filling is set and has a slight jiggle in the center.

Cool:
- Allow the lemon tart to cool completely in the tart pan.

Serve:

Dust with Powdered Sugar:
- Dust the cooled lemon tart with powdered sugar.

Garnish (Optional):
- Garnish with fresh berries if desired.

Slice and Enjoy:
- Slice and serve the lemon tart. It can be served chilled or at room temperature.

Tips:

- For a decorative touch, you can create a lattice pattern on top of the tart with strips of additional tart dough before baking.
- Adjust the amount of sugar in the filling based on your preference for sweetness.

Enjoy your delightful and tangy Lemon Tart!

Nutella Pastry Twists

Ingredients:

- 1 sheet puff pastry, thawed if frozen
- 1/2 cup Nutella or any chocolate hazelnut spread
- 1 egg (for egg wash)
- Powdered sugar for dusting (optional)

Instructions:

Preheat Oven:
- Preheat your oven to 375°F (190°C). Line a baking sheet with parchment paper.

Roll Out Puff Pastry:
- On a lightly floured surface, roll out the puff pastry sheet into a large rectangle.

Spread Nutella:
- Evenly spread Nutella over the entire surface of the puff pastry.

Fold and Seal:
- Fold the puff pastry in half lengthwise, covering the Nutella. Press the edges to seal.

Cut Into Strips:
- Using a sharp knife or a pizza cutter, cut the folded pastry into strips about 1/2 to 1 inch wide.

Twist the Strips:
- Twist each strip several times to create a spiral pattern.

Place on Baking Sheet:
- Place the twisted pastry strips on the prepared baking sheet, leaving some space between each twist.

Make Egg Wash:
- In a small bowl, beat the egg. Brush the egg wash over the top of each pastry twist.

Bake:
- Bake in the preheated oven for 12-15 minutes or until the twists are golden brown and puffed.

Cool:
- Allow the Nutella pastry twists to cool on the baking sheet for a few minutes before transferring them to a wire rack to cool completely.

Optional: Dust with Powdered Sugar:
- If desired, dust the cooled twists with powdered sugar before serving.

Tips:

- You can add a sprinkle of chopped nuts or a drizzle of melted chocolate over the twists for extra flavor and decoration.
- Serve the Nutella pastry twists warm for a gooey and delicious treat.

Enjoy these Nutella Pastry Twists as a delightful snack or dessert!

Raspberry Linzer Cookies

Ingredients:

For the Cookies:

- 1 cup unsalted butter, softened
- 2/3 cup granulated sugar
- 1 teaspoon vanilla extract
- 2 cups all-purpose flour
- 1 cup ground almonds or almond flour
- 1/2 teaspoon ground cinnamon
- 1/4 teaspoon salt
- 1/2 cup raspberry jam or preserves

For Dusting:

- Powdered sugar

Instructions:

Prepare the Dough:

    Cream Butter and Sugar:
- In a large bowl, cream together the softened butter and granulated sugar until light and fluffy.

    Add Vanilla:
- Mix in the vanilla extract.

    Combine Dry Ingredients:
- In a separate bowl, whisk together the all-purpose flour, ground almonds, ground cinnamon, and salt.

    Add Dry Ingredients to Wet Ingredients:
- Gradually add the dry ingredients to the wet ingredients, mixing until the dough comes together.

    Divide and Chill:
- Divide the dough into two equal portions, shape each into a disk, wrap in plastic wrap, and refrigerate for at least 1 hour or until firm.

Roll and Cut Cookies:

Preheat Oven:
- Preheat your oven to 350°F (175°C). Line baking sheets with parchment paper.

Roll Out Dough:
- On a floured surface, roll out one portion of the chilled dough to about 1/8 inch thickness.

Cut Shapes:
- Use a round or heart-shaped cookie cutter to cut out cookies. For half of the cookies, use a smaller cutter to create a window in the center.

Bake:
- Place the cookies on the prepared baking sheets and bake for 10-12 minutes or until the edges are lightly golden. Repeat with the remaining portion of dough.

Cool:
- Allow the cookies to cool on the baking sheets for a few minutes before transferring them to wire racks to cool completely.

Assemble the Cookies:

Spread Jam:
- On the solid cookies (without the center cutout), spread a thin layer of raspberry jam.

Top with Windowed Cookies:
- Place the cookies with the center cutout on top of the jam-covered cookies to create a sandwich.

Dust with Powdered Sugar:
- Dust the tops of the assembled Raspberry Linzer Cookies with powdered sugar.

Tips:

- If the jam is too thick, you can heat it slightly to make it easier to spread on the cookies.
- Experiment with different fruit preserves or jams to create variations of the Linzer cookies.

Enjoy these delightful Raspberry Linzer Cookies with a cup of tea or coffee!

Baklava

Ingredients:

For the Filling:

- 1 1/2 cups mixed nuts (such as walnuts, pistachios, and almonds), finely chopped
- 1/4 cup granulated sugar
- 1 teaspoon ground cinnamon

For the Phyllo Layers:

- 1 package (16 ounces) phyllo dough, thawed according to package instructions
- 1 cup unsalted butter, melted

For the Syrup:

- 1 cup water
- 1 cup granulated sugar
- 1/2 cup honey
- 1 cinnamon stick
- 1 teaspoon vanilla extract
- Zest of 1 lemon

Instructions:

Prepare the Filling:

    Chop Nuts:
- In a food processor, pulse the mixed nuts until finely chopped. Be careful not to over-process, as you want a coarse texture.

    Add Sugar and Cinnamon:
- Transfer the chopped nuts to a bowl and mix in the granulated sugar and ground cinnamon. Set aside.

Prepare the Phyllo Dough:

    Preheat Oven:

- Preheat your oven to 350°F (175°C). Grease a baking dish (usually around 9x13 inches).

Layer Phyllo Sheets:
- Lay one sheet of phyllo dough in the prepared dish, brush it with melted butter, and repeat until you have 8-10 layers.

Add Nut Filling:
- Sprinkle a generous portion of the nut mixture over the phyllo layers.

Continue Layering:
- Add 4-6 more layers of phyllo, brushing each layer with melted butter.

Add Another Layer of Nuts:
- Sprinkle another layer of the nut mixture on top.

Finish with Phyllo Layers:
- Continue layering the remaining phyllo sheets, brushing each with melted butter.

Score the Baklava:
- Using a sharp knife, score the baklava into diamond or square shapes. This will make it easier to cut after baking.

Bake:
- Bake in the preheated oven for 40-45 minutes or until the baklava is golden brown and crisp.

Make the Syrup:

Combine Ingredients:
- In a saucepan, combine water, sugar, honey, cinnamon stick, vanilla extract, and lemon zest. Bring to a boil, then reduce heat and simmer for about 15 minutes.

Strain Syrup:
- Remove the cinnamon stick and strain the syrup to remove any lemon zest.

Pour Syrup Over Baklava:

Cool Slightly:
- Allow the baked baklava to cool for a few minutes.

Pour Syrup:
- Pour the warm syrup evenly over the baklava.

Let it Absorb:
- Allow the baklava to absorb the syrup and cool completely before serving.

Serve:

> Cut and Enjoy:
> - Once fully cooled, cut the baklava along the scored lines and serve.

Tips:

- To prevent the phyllo dough from drying out, cover it with a damp kitchen towel while working with it.
- Baklava is often best when it has had time to sit and absorb the syrup, so consider making it a day ahead for optimal flavor.

Enjoy the rich and sweet taste of homemade Baklava!

Mini Quiches

Ingredients:

For the Crust:

- 1 1/4 cups all-purpose flour
- 1/2 cup unsalted butter, cold and cut into small cubes
- 1/4 teaspoon salt
- 1/4 cup cold water

For the Filling:

- 1 cup milk
- 4 large eggs
- Salt and pepper to taste
- 1 cup grated cheese (such as Swiss, cheddar, or Gruyere)
- 1/2 cup diced ham or cooked bacon
- 1/4 cup finely chopped onion
- 1/4 cup chopped fresh spinach or other veggies of your choice

Instructions:

Prepare the Crust:

Combine Ingredients:
- In a food processor, combine the flour, cold butter cubes, and salt. Pulse until the mixture resembles coarse crumbs.

Add Cold Water:
- With the food processor running, gradually add the cold water until the dough comes together.

Form Dough:
- Turn the dough out onto a lightly floured surface and shape it into a disc. Wrap in plastic wrap and refrigerate for at least 30 minutes.

Preheat Oven:
- Preheat your oven to 375°F (190°C). Grease a mini muffin tin.

Roll Out Dough:

- On a floured surface, roll out the chilled dough to about 1/8 inch thickness.

Cut Circles:
- Use a round cookie cutter or a glass to cut circles from the rolled-out dough. Press each circle into the mini muffin tin, forming mini crusts.

Prepare the Filling:

Whisk Eggs and Milk:
- In a bowl, whisk together the eggs and milk. Season with salt and pepper.

Add Cheese and Fillings:
- Stir in the grated cheese, diced ham or bacon, chopped onion, and chopped spinach or other veggies.

Assemble and Bake:

Fill the Crusts:
- Spoon the egg and filling mixture into each mini crust.

Bake:
- Bake in the preheated oven for 12-15 minutes or until the quiches are set and golden brown.

Cool and Serve:
- Allow the mini quiches to cool in the muffin tin for a few minutes before transferring them to a wire rack.

Serve:

Serve Warm or at Room Temperature:
- Mini quiches can be served warm or at room temperature.

Garnish (Optional):
- Garnish with fresh herbs or a sprinkle of grated cheese before serving.

Tips:

- Customize the filling based on your preferences, adding ingredients like mushrooms, bell peppers, or different types of cheese.
- These mini quiches are great for parties, brunches, or as a grab-and-go snack.

Enjoy these delicious and versatile Mini Quiches!

Pecan Pie Bars

Ingredients:

For the Crust:

- 1 1/2 cups all-purpose flour
- 1/2 cup unsalted butter, cold and cut into small cubes
- 1/4 cup granulated sugar
- 1/4 teaspoon salt

For the Pecan Filling:

- 3/4 cup unsalted butter
- 1/2 cup granulated sugar
- 1 cup light corn syrup
- 4 large eggs, beaten
- 1 teaspoon vanilla extract
- 2 1/2 cups chopped pecans

Instructions:

Prepare the Crust:

Preheat Oven:
- Preheat your oven to 350°F (175°C). Line a 9x13-inch baking pan with parchment paper, leaving some overhang on the sides for easy removal.

Combine Crust Ingredients:
- In a food processor, combine the flour, cold butter cubes, granulated sugar, and salt. Pulse until the mixture resembles coarse crumbs.

Form Dough:
- Press the mixture into the bottom of the prepared baking pan to form an even crust layer.

Bake Crust:
- Bake the crust in the preheated oven for 15-20 minutes or until it is lightly golden. Remove from the oven and set aside.

Prepare the Pecan Filling:

- Melt Butter:
    - In a saucepan over medium heat, melt the butter.
- Add Sugar and Corn Syrup:
    - Stir in the granulated sugar and light corn syrup. Bring the mixture to a simmer, stirring constantly. Remove from heat once the sugar is dissolved.
- Cool Slightly:
    - Allow the sugar mixture to cool slightly.
- Add Beaten Eggs and Vanilla:
    - Gradually whisk the beaten eggs into the sugar mixture. Stir in the vanilla extract.
- Stir in Chopped Pecans:
    - Fold in the chopped pecans until evenly distributed.

Assemble and Bake:

- Pour Pecan Filling Over Crust:
    - Pour the pecan filling evenly over the pre-baked crust.
- Bake Again:
    - Bake in the preheated oven for 25-30 minutes or until the pecan filling is set and golden brown.
- Cool Completely:
    - Allow the pecan pie bars to cool completely in the baking pan.

Serve:

- Remove from Pan:
    - Use the parchment paper overhang to lift the pecan pie bars out of the pan.
- Cut into Bars:
    - Place the bars on a cutting board and cut into squares or bars.
- Optional: Dust with Powdered Sugar:
    - If desired, dust the pecan pie bars with powdered sugar before serving.

Tips:

- For an extra layer of flavor, consider adding a pinch of cinnamon or a splash of bourbon to the pecan filling.
- Serve these pecan pie bars with a dollop of whipped cream or a scoop of vanilla ice cream for a delightful treat.

Enjoy these delicious Pecan Pie Bars, a perfect alternative to traditional pecan pie!

Cakes:

Classic Vanilla Cake

Ingredients:

For the Cake:

- 2 1/2 cups all-purpose flour
- 2 1/2 teaspoons baking powder
- 1/2 teaspoon salt
- 1 cup unsalted butter, softened
- 2 cups granulated sugar
- 4 large eggs
- 2 teaspoons vanilla extract
- 1 1/2 cups whole milk

For the Vanilla Buttercream Frosting:

- 1 cup unsalted butter, softened
- 4 cups powdered sugar
- 1/4 cup whole milk
- 2 teaspoons vanilla extract
- Pinch of salt

Instructions:

For the Cake:

Preheat Oven:
- Preheat your oven to 350°F (175°C). Grease and flour two 9-inch round cake pans.

Combine Dry Ingredients:
- In a bowl, whisk together the flour, baking powder, and salt. Set aside.

Cream Butter and Sugar:
- In a large mixing bowl, cream together the softened butter and granulated sugar until light and fluffy.

Add Eggs and Vanilla:

- Add the eggs one at a time, beating well after each addition. Stir in the vanilla extract.

Alternate Adding Dry Ingredients and Milk:
- Gradually add the dry ingredients to the butter mixture, alternating with the milk. Begin and end with the dry ingredients, mixing just until combined.

Divide Batter and Bake:
- Divide the batter evenly between the prepared cake pans. Smooth the tops with a spatula. Bake in the preheated oven for 25-30 minutes or until a toothpick inserted into the center comes out clean.

Cool:
- Allow the cakes to cool in the pans for 10 minutes, then transfer them to a wire rack to cool completely.

For the Vanilla Buttercream Frosting:

Beat Butter:
- In a large bowl, beat the softened butter until creamy and smooth.

Add Powdered Sugar:
- Gradually add the powdered sugar, beating well after each addition.

Add Milk and Vanilla:
- Pour in the milk and vanilla extract. Beat until the frosting is smooth and fluffy. Add a pinch of salt to balance the sweetness.

Assemble and Frost the Cake:

Level Cakes (Optional):
- If needed, level the cooled cakes using a serrated knife or cake leveler.

Place First Cake Layer:
- Place one cake layer on a serving platter or cake stand.

Spread Frosting:
- Spread a layer of vanilla buttercream frosting over the top of the first cake layer.

Add Second Cake Layer:
- Place the second cake layer on top, creating a two-layer cake.

Frost the Top and Sides:
- Frost the top and sides of the entire cake with the vanilla buttercream frosting. Use a spatula to create a smooth finish.

Decorate (Optional):

- Decorate the cake as desired with additional frosting, sprinkles, or other decorations.

Slice and Serve:
- Slice and serve the classic vanilla cake. Enjoy!

Tips:

- For a more intense vanilla flavor, consider using vanilla bean paste or scraping the seeds from a vanilla bean into the cake batter and frosting.
- Ensure the cakes are completely cooled before frosting to prevent the frosting from melting.

This Classic Vanilla Cake is a timeless treat perfect for any celebration or simply satisfying your sweet tooth!

Chocolate Layer Cake

Ingredients:

For the Chocolate Cake:

- 2 cups all-purpose flour
- 1 3/4 cups granulated sugar
- 3/4 cup unsweetened cocoa powder
- 2 teaspoons baking powder
- 1 1/2 teaspoons baking soda
- 1 teaspoon salt
- 2 large eggs
- 1 cup whole milk
- 1/2 cup vegetable oil
- 2 teaspoons vanilla extract
- 1 cup boiling water

For the Chocolate Buttercream Frosting:

- 1 1/2 cups unsalted butter, softened
- 3 1/2 cups powdered sugar
- 1 cup unsweetened cocoa powder
- 1/2 cup whole milk
- 2 teaspoons vanilla extract
- Pinch of salt

Instructions:

For the Chocolate Cake:

Preheat Oven:
- Preheat your oven to 350°F (175°C). Grease and flour two 9-inch round cake pans.

Combine Dry Ingredients:
- In a large mixing bowl, sift together the flour, sugar, cocoa powder, baking powder, baking soda, and salt.

Add Wet Ingredients:
- Add the eggs, milk, vegetable oil, and vanilla extract to the dry ingredients. Mix until well combined.

Add Boiling Water:
- Gradually add the boiling water to the batter, mixing well. The batter will be thin, but that's okay.

Pour into Pans:
- Pour the batter evenly into the prepared cake pans.

Bake:
- Bake in the preheated oven for 30-35 minutes or until a toothpick inserted into the center comes out clean.

Cool:
- Allow the cakes to cool in the pans for 10 minutes, then transfer them to a wire rack to cool completely.

For the Chocolate Buttercream Frosting:

Beat Butter:
- In a large bowl, beat the softened butter until creamy and smooth.

Add Dry Ingredients:
- Sift in the powdered sugar and cocoa powder. Mix on low speed until combined.

Add Milk and Vanilla:
- Pour in the milk and vanilla extract. Beat on medium speed until the frosting is smooth and fluffy. Add a pinch of salt to balance the sweetness.

Assemble and Frost the Cake:

Level Cakes (Optional):
- If needed, level the cooled cakes using a serrated knife or cake leveler.

Place First Cake Layer:
- Place one cake layer on a serving platter or cake stand.

Spread Frosting:
- Spread a layer of chocolate buttercream frosting over the top of the first cake layer.

Add Second Cake Layer:
- Place the second cake layer on top, creating a two-layer cake.

Frost the Top and Sides:
- Frost the top and sides of the entire cake with the chocolate buttercream frosting. Use a spatula to create a smooth finish.

Decorate (Optional):

- Decorate the cake as desired with additional frosting, chocolate shavings, or other decorations.

Slice and Serve:
- Slice and serve the decadent chocolate layer cake. Enjoy!

Tips:

- For an extra rich chocolate flavor, consider using dark cocoa powder in both the cake and frosting.
- You can add chocolate ganache between the cake layers for an extra indulgent touch.

This Chocolate Layer Cake is a chocolate lover's dream, perfect for special occasions or any day you crave a rich and moist chocolate treat!

Lemon Blueberry Bundt Cake

Ingredients:

For the Cake:

- 3 cups all-purpose flour
- 1 teaspoon baking powder
- 1/2 teaspoon baking soda
- 1/2 teaspoon salt
- 1 cup unsalted butter, softened
- 2 cups granulated sugar
- 4 large eggs
- 1 teaspoon vanilla extract
- 1 cup sour cream
- Zest of 2 lemons
- 1/4 cup fresh lemon juice
- 2 cups fresh or frozen blueberries (if using frozen, toss them in a bit of flour to prevent sinking)

For the Glaze:

- 1 cup powdered sugar
- 2 tablespoons fresh lemon juice
- Zest of 1 lemon

Instructions:

For the Cake:

> Preheat Oven:
> - Preheat your oven to 350°F (175°C). Grease and flour a bundt cake pan.
>
> Combine Dry Ingredients:
> - In a bowl, whisk together the flour, baking powder, baking soda, and salt. Set aside.
>
> Cream Butter and Sugar:

- In a large mixing bowl, cream together the softened butter and granulated sugar until light and fluffy.

Add Eggs and Vanilla:
- Add the eggs one at a time, beating well after each addition. Stir in the vanilla extract.

Add Sour Cream and Lemon Zest:
- Mix in the sour cream and lemon zest until well combined.

Add Dry Ingredients Alternately with Lemon Juice:
- Gradually add the dry ingredients to the wet ingredients, alternating with the fresh lemon juice. Begin and end with the dry ingredients. Mix just until combined.

Fold in Blueberries:
- Gently fold in the blueberries until evenly distributed.

Bake:
- Pour the batter into the prepared bundt pan and smooth the top. Bake in the preheated oven for 50-60 minutes or until a toothpick inserted into the center comes out clean.

Cool:
- Allow the cake to cool in the pan for 15 minutes, then transfer it to a wire rack to cool completely.

For the Glaze:

Mix Glaze Ingredients:
- In a small bowl, whisk together the powdered sugar, fresh lemon juice, and lemon zest until smooth.

Glaze the Cake:
- Once the cake has cooled, drizzle the lemon glaze over the top of the bundt cake.

Let Glaze Set:
- Allow the glaze to set before slicing and serving.

Serve:

Slice and Enjoy:
- Slice and serve the delicious Lemon Blueberry Bundt Cake. Optionally, garnish with additional lemon zest or fresh blueberries.

Tips:

- If using frozen blueberries, coat them in a bit of flour before folding them into the batter to prevent them from sinking to the bottom of the cake.
- Ensure the cake is completely cool before applying the glaze for the best texture.

Enjoy this delightful Lemon Blueberry Bundt Cake, perfect for any occasion or as a sweet treat with your favorite cup of tea or coffee!

Carrot Cake with Cream Cheese Frosting

Ingredients:

For the Carrot Cake:

- 2 cups all-purpose flour
- 2 cups granulated sugar
- 1 teaspoon baking powder
- 1/2 teaspoon baking soda
- 1/2 teaspoon salt
- 1 teaspoon ground cinnamon
- 1/2 teaspoon ground nutmeg
- 1/2 teaspoon ground ginger
- 1 cup vegetable oil
- 4 large eggs
- 2 teaspoons vanilla extract
- 2 cups finely grated carrots
- 1 cup crushed pineapple, drained
- 1/2 cup shredded coconut (optional)
- 1/2 cup chopped nuts (walnuts or pecans), optional

For the Cream Cheese Frosting:

- 8 ounces cream cheese, softened
- 1/2 cup unsalted butter, softened
- 4 cups powdered sugar
- 1 teaspoon vanilla extract

Instructions:

For the Carrot Cake:

   Preheat Oven:
   - Preheat your oven to 350°F (175°C). Grease and flour two 9-inch round cake pans.

   Combine Dry Ingredients:

- In a bowl, whisk together the flour, sugar, baking powder, baking soda, salt, cinnamon, nutmeg, and ginger.

Mix Wet Ingredients:
- In a separate large mixing bowl, whisk together the vegetable oil, eggs, and vanilla extract until well combined.

Add Dry Ingredients:
- Gradually add the dry ingredients to the wet ingredients, mixing until just combined.

Fold in Carrots, Pineapple, Coconut, and Nuts:
- Gently fold in the finely grated carrots, crushed pineapple, shredded coconut (if using), and chopped nuts (if using) until evenly distributed.

Divide Batter and Bake:
- Divide the batter equally between the prepared cake pans. Smooth the tops with a spatula. Bake in the preheated oven for 25-30 minutes or until a toothpick inserted into the center comes out clean.

Cool:
- Allow the cakes to cool in the pans for 10 minutes, then transfer them to a wire rack to cool completely.

For the Cream Cheese Frosting:

Beat Cream Cheese and Butter:
- In a large bowl, beat together the softened cream cheese and butter until creamy and smooth.

Add Powdered Sugar and Vanilla:
- Gradually add the powdered sugar, beating well after each addition. Mix in the vanilla extract until smooth.

Assemble and Frost the Cake:

Level Cakes (Optional):
- If needed, level the cooled cakes using a serrated knife or cake leveler.

Place First Cake Layer:
- Place one cake layer on a serving platter or cake stand.

Spread Cream Cheese Frosting:
- Spread a layer of cream cheese frosting over the top of the first cake layer.

Add Second Cake Layer:
- Place the second cake layer on top, creating a two-layer cake.

Frost the Top and Sides:
- Frost the top and sides of the entire cake with the cream cheese frosting. Use a spatula to create a smooth finish.

Decorate (Optional):
- Decorate the cake as desired with additional frosting, chopped nuts, or shredded carrots.

Chill (Optional):
- For best results, chill the carrot cake in the refrigerator for an hour before slicing and serving.

Serve:

Slice and Enjoy:
- Slice and serve the delicious Carrot Cake with Cream Cheese Frosting.

Tips:

- Adjust the amount of powdered sugar in the frosting to achieve your desired level of sweetness.
- You can add a touch of orange zest to the cream cheese frosting for an extra burst of flavor.

Enjoy this moist and flavorful Carrot Cake with luscious Cream Cheese Frosting, a classic favorite for any celebration!

Almond Joy Cake

Ingredients:

For the Cake:

- 2 cups all-purpose flour
- 1 3/4 cups granulated sugar
- 3/4 cup unsweetened cocoa powder
- 2 teaspoons baking powder
- 1/2 teaspoon baking soda
- 1/2 teaspoon salt
- 1 cup vegetable oil
- 4 large eggs
- 2 teaspoons vanilla extract
- 1 1/2 cups buttermilk

For the Coconut Filling:

- 1 can (14 ounces) sweetened condensed milk
- 1 1/2 cups sweetened shredded coconut
- 1/2 cup chopped almonds

For the Chocolate Ganache:

- 1 cup semi-sweet chocolate chips
- 1/2 cup heavy cream
- 1 tablespoon unsalted butter

For Garnish:

- Additional shredded coconut
- Chopped almonds

Instructions:

For the Cake:

    Preheat Oven:

- Preheat your oven to 350°F (175°C). Grease and flour three 8-inch round cake pans.

Combine Dry Ingredients:
- In a bowl, whisk together the flour, sugar, cocoa powder, baking powder, baking soda, and salt.

Mix Wet Ingredients:
- In a separate large mixing bowl, whisk together the vegetable oil, eggs, and vanilla extract until well combined.

Add Dry Ingredients Alternately with Buttermilk:
- Gradually add the dry ingredients to the wet ingredients, alternating with the buttermilk. Begin and end with the dry ingredients. Mix just until combined.

Divide Batter and Bake:
- Divide the batter equally between the prepared cake pans. Smooth the tops with a spatula. Bake in the preheated oven for 25-30 minutes or until a toothpick inserted into the center comes out clean.

Cool:
- Allow the cakes to cool in the pans for 10 minutes, then transfer them to a wire rack to cool completely.

For the Coconut Filling:

Mix Filling Ingredients:
- In a bowl, mix together the sweetened condensed milk, shredded coconut, and chopped almonds.

For the Chocolate Ganache:

Heat Chocolate Chips and Cream:
- In a heatproof bowl, combine the chocolate chips and heavy cream. Heat in the microwave or over a double boiler until the cream is hot. Stir until the chocolate is melted and smooth. Mix in the unsalted butter.

Assemble the Almond Joy Cake:

Level Cakes (Optional):
- If needed, level the cooled cakes using a serrated knife or cake leveler.

Place First Cake Layer:
- Place one cake layer on a serving platter or cake stand.

Spread Coconut Filling:
- Spread a layer of the coconut filling over the top of the first cake layer.

Add Second Cake Layer:
- Place the second cake layer on top, pressing down gently.

Repeat Filling and Add Third Cake Layer:
- Spread another layer of the coconut filling over the second cake layer, then place the third cake layer on top.

Frost with Chocolate Ganache:
- Pour the chocolate ganache over the top of the cake, allowing it to drip down the sides.

Garnish:
- Garnish the top of the cake with additional shredded coconut and chopped almonds.

Chill (Optional):
- For best results, chill the Almond Joy Cake in the refrigerator for an hour before slicing and serving.

Serve:

Slice and Enjoy:
- Slice and serve the decadent Almond Joy Cake.

Tips:

- Toast the shredded coconut and almonds for additional flavor before adding them to the filling or garnishing the cake.
- For a more intense almond flavor, consider adding almond extract to the cake batter or the coconut filling.

Enjoy the rich and indulgent taste of this Almond Joy Cake, inspired by the classic candy bar!

Red Wine Chocolate Cake

Ingredients:

For the Cake:

- 1 3/4 cups all-purpose flour
- 1 3/4 cups granulated sugar
- 3/4 cup unsweetened cocoa powder
- 2 teaspoons baking soda
- 1 teaspoon baking powder
- 1 teaspoon salt
- 2 large eggs
- 1 cup whole milk
- 1/2 cup vegetable oil
- 2 teaspoons vanilla extract
- 1 cup red wine (choose a good-quality red wine with flavors you enjoy)

For the Chocolate Ganache:

- 1 cup semi-sweet chocolate chips
- 1/2 cup heavy cream
- 1 tablespoon unsalted butter

For Garnish:

- Powdered sugar
- Fresh berries (optional)

Instructions:

For the Cake:

    Preheat Oven:
- Preheat your oven to 350°F (175°C). Grease and flour two 9-inch round cake pans.

    Combine Dry Ingredients:

- In a bowl, whisk together the flour, sugar, cocoa powder, baking soda, baking powder, and salt.

Mix Wet Ingredients:
- In a separate large mixing bowl, whisk together the eggs, milk, vegetable oil, and vanilla extract until well combined.

Add Dry Ingredients Alternately with Red Wine:
- Gradually add the dry ingredients to the wet ingredients, alternating with the red wine. Begin and end with the dry ingredients. Mix just until combined.

Divide Batter and Bake:
- Divide the batter equally between the prepared cake pans. Smooth the tops with a spatula. Bake in the preheated oven for 25-30 minutes or until a toothpick inserted into the center comes out clean.

Cool:
- Allow the cakes to cool in the pans for 10 minutes, then transfer them to a wire rack to cool completely.

For the Chocolate Ganache:

Heat Chocolate Chips and Cream:
- In a heatproof bowl, combine the chocolate chips and heavy cream. Heat in the microwave or over a double boiler until the cream is hot. Stir until the chocolate is melted and smooth. Mix in the unsalted butter.

Assemble the Red Wine Chocolate Cake:

Level Cakes (Optional):
- If needed, level the cooled cakes using a serrated knife or cake leveler.

Place First Cake Layer:
- Place one cake layer on a serving platter or cake stand.

Pour Chocolate Ganache:
- Pour a generous amount of the chocolate ganache over the top of the first cake layer.

Add Second Cake Layer:
- Place the second cake layer on top, pressing down gently.

Cover with Ganache:
- Pour the remaining chocolate ganache over the top of the cake, allowing it to drip down the sides.

Garnish:
- Garnish the top of the cake with a dusting of powdered sugar and fresh berries if desired.

Serve:

Slice and Enjoy:
- Slice and serve the rich and decadent Red Wine Chocolate Cake.

Tips:

- Choose a red wine with flavors that complement chocolate, such as Cabernet Sauvignon or Merlot.
- For added richness, consider adding a layer of chocolate mousse or ganache between the cake layers.

Indulge in the luxurious flavor combination of red wine and chocolate with this delicious Red Wine Chocolate Cake!

Tiramisu Cake

Ingredients:

For the Cake:

- 2 cups all-purpose flour
- 2 teaspoons baking powder
- 1/2 teaspoon baking soda
- 1/4 teaspoon salt
- 1/2 cup unsalted butter, softened
- 1 1/2 cups granulated sugar
- 4 large eggs
- 1 teaspoon vanilla extract
- 1 cup sour cream

For the Coffee Soaking Syrup:

- 1 cup strong brewed coffee, cooled
- 2 tablespoons coffee liqueur (optional)
- 1/4 cup granulated sugar

For the Mascarpone Filling:

- 8 ounces mascarpone cheese, softened
- 1 cup powdered sugar
- 1 teaspoon vanilla extract
- 1 1/2 cups heavy cream, whipped to stiff peaks

For Garnish:

- Unsweetened cocoa powder
- Chocolate shavings

Instructions:

For the Cake:

   Preheat Oven:

- Preheat your oven to 350°F (175°C). Grease and flour two 9-inch round cake pans.

Combine Dry Ingredients:
- In a bowl, whisk together the flour, baking powder, baking soda, and salt.

Cream Butter and Sugar:
- In a large mixing bowl, cream together the softened butter and granulated sugar until light and fluffy.

Add Eggs and Vanilla:
- Add the eggs one at a time, beating well after each addition. Stir in the vanilla extract.

Add Dry Ingredients Alternately with Sour Cream:
- Gradually add the dry ingredients to the butter mixture, alternating with the sour cream. Begin and end with the dry ingredients. Mix just until combined.

Divide Batter and Bake:
- Divide the batter equally between the prepared cake pans. Smooth the tops with a spatula. Bake in the preheated oven for 25-30 minutes or until a toothpick inserted into the center comes out clean.

Cool:
- Allow the cakes to cool in the pans for 10 minutes, then transfer them to a wire rack to cool completely.

For the Coffee Soaking Syrup:

Mix Ingredients:
- In a bowl, mix together the brewed coffee, coffee liqueur (if using), and granulated sugar until the sugar is dissolved.

For the Mascarpone Filling:

Beat Mascarpone, Sugar, and Vanilla:
- In a bowl, beat together the softened mascarpone cheese, powdered sugar, and vanilla extract until smooth.

Fold in Whipped Cream:
- Gently fold in the whipped heavy cream until well combined. Be careful not to deflate the whipped cream.

Assemble the Tiramisu Cake:

Level Cakes (Optional):
- If needed, level the cooled cakes using a serrated knife or cake leveler.

Place First Cake Layer:
- Place one cake layer on a serving platter or cake stand.

Soak with Coffee Syrup:
- Using a pastry brush, generously soak the top of the first cake layer with the coffee soaking syrup.

Spread Mascarpone Filling:
- Spread a layer of the mascarpone filling over the soaked cake layer.

Add Second Cake Layer:
- Place the second cake layer on top.

Repeat Soaking and Filling:
- Repeat the process by soaking the second cake layer with the coffee syrup and spreading another layer of the mascarpone filling.

Frost Top and Sides:
- Use the remaining mascarpone filling to frost the top and sides of the entire cake.

Garnish:
- Dust the top of the cake with unsweetened cocoa powder and garnish with chocolate shavings.

Serve:

Chill (Optional):
- For the best flavor, chill the Tiramisu Cake in the refrigerator for a few hours before serving.

Slice and Enjoy:
- Slice and serve this delightful Tiramisu Cake with layers of coffee-soaked cake and luscious mascarpone filling.

Tips:

- Adjust the amount of coffee syrup based on your preference for the level of coffee flavor.
- Make sure the mascarpone cheese is softened to room temperature for smooth incorporation into the filling.

Indulge in the classic flavors of Tiramisu with this decadent Tiramisu Cake!

Pineapple Upside-Down Cake

Ingredients:

For the Topping:

- 1/2 cup unsalted butter
- 1 cup packed brown sugar
- 1 can (20 ounces) pineapple slices in juice, drained (reserve the juice)
- Maraschino cherries, for garnish

For the Cake:

- 1 1/2 cups all-purpose flour
- 1 1/2 teaspoons baking powder
- 1/4 teaspoon salt
- 1/2 cup unsalted butter, softened
- 1 cup granulated sugar
- 2 large eggs
- 1 teaspoon vanilla extract
- 1/2 cup pineapple juice (reserved from the canned pineapple)
- 1/2 cup whole milk

Instructions:

For the Topping:

    Preheat Oven:
- Preheat your oven to 350°F (175°C).

    Melt Butter:
- In a 9-inch round cake pan, melt the unsalted butter over low heat.

    Add Brown Sugar:
- Sprinkle the packed brown sugar evenly over the melted butter in the cake pan. Stir to combine until the sugar is dissolved.

    Arrange Pineapple Slices:
- Arrange the pineapple slices on top of the brown sugar mixture in the cake pan. Place a maraschino cherry in the center of each pineapple ring and in the spaces between the rings.

For the Cake:

Combine Dry Ingredients:
- In a bowl, whisk together the all-purpose flour, baking powder, and salt.

Cream Butter and Sugar:
- In a separate large mixing bowl, cream together the softened butter and granulated sugar until light and fluffy.

Add Eggs and Vanilla:
- Add the eggs one at a time, beating well after each addition. Stir in the vanilla extract.

Add Dry Ingredients Alternately with Liquids:
- Gradually add the dry ingredients to the butter mixture, alternating with the pineapple juice and milk. Begin and end with the dry ingredients. Mix just until combined.

Pour Batter Over Topping:
- Pour the cake batter evenly over the arranged pineapple slices in the cake pan.

Bake:
- Bake in the preheated oven for 30-35 minutes or until a toothpick inserted into the center of the cake comes out clean.

Cool and Invert:
- Allow the cake to cool in the pan for 10 minutes. Place a serving plate over the cake pan and invert the cake onto the plate. Carefully lift the pan to reveal the pineapple topping.

Cool Completely:
- Allow the cake to cool completely before serving.

Serve:

Slice and Enjoy:
- Slice and serve the delicious Pineapple Upside-Down Cake. It's wonderful when served warm or at room temperature.

Tips:

- Customize the topping by adding pecans or walnuts between the pineapple rings for extra crunch.
- Serve with a dollop of whipped cream or a scoop of vanilla ice cream for a delightful treat.

Enjoy the nostalgic and sweet flavors of Pineapple Upside-Down Cake with this simple and classic recipe!

Coconut Lime Pound Cake

Ingredients:

For the Cake:

- 1 cup unsalted butter, softened
- 2 cups granulated sugar
- 4 large eggs
- 3 cups all-purpose flour
- 1 teaspoon baking powder
- 1/2 teaspoon baking soda
- 1/2 teaspoon salt
- 1 cup coconut milk
- 1/4 cup fresh lime juice
- Zest of 2 limes
- 1 teaspoon vanilla extract

For the Glaze:

- 1 cup powdered sugar
- 2 tablespoons fresh lime juice
- Zest of 1 lime
- 1/4 cup shredded coconut, toasted (for garnish)

Instructions:

For the Coconut Lime Pound Cake:

Preheat Oven:
- Preheat your oven to 350°F (175°C). Grease and flour a bundt cake pan.

Cream Butter and Sugar:
- In a large mixing bowl, cream together the softened butter and granulated sugar until light and fluffy.

Add Eggs:
- Add the eggs one at a time, beating well after each addition.

Combine Dry Ingredients:
- In a separate bowl, whisk together the flour, baking powder, baking soda, and salt.

Add Dry Ingredients Alternately with Liquids:

- Gradually add the dry ingredients to the butter mixture, alternating with the coconut milk. Begin and end with the dry ingredients. Mix just until combined.

Add Lime Juice, Zest, and Vanilla:
- Stir in the fresh lime juice, lime zest, and vanilla extract until well incorporated.

Pour Batter into Pan:
- Pour the batter into the prepared bundt cake pan, spreading it evenly.

Bake:
- Bake in the preheated oven for 50-60 minutes or until a toothpick inserted into the center comes out clean.

Cool:
- Allow the cake to cool in the pan for 15 minutes, then transfer it to a wire rack to cool completely.

For the Glaze:

Mix Glaze Ingredients:
- In a bowl, whisk together the powdered sugar, fresh lime juice, and lime zest until smooth.

Glaze the Cake:
- Once the cake has cooled, drizzle the lime glaze over the top of the bundt cake.

Toast Coconut:
- In a dry skillet over medium heat, toast the shredded coconut until golden brown. Keep an eye on it, as it can burn quickly.

Garnish:
- Garnish the glazed cake with toasted shredded coconut.

Serve:

Slice and Enjoy:
- Slice and serve the delicious Coconut Lime Pound Cake. It pairs well with a cup of tea or coffee.

Tips:

- Make sure the ingredients, especially the coconut milk, lime juice, and lime zest, are at room temperature for better incorporation into the batter.

- Adjust the glaze consistency by adding more powdered sugar or lime juice, as needed.

Enjoy the tropical flavors of coconut and lime in this delightful Coconut Lime Pound Cake!

Black Forest Cake

Ingredients:

For the Chocolate Cake:

- 2 cups all-purpose flour
- 2 cups granulated sugar
- 3/4 cup unsweetened cocoa powder
- 2 teaspoons baking powder
- 1 1/2 teaspoons baking soda
- 1 teaspoon salt
- 2 large eggs
- 1 cup whole milk
- 1/2 cup vegetable oil
- 2 teaspoons vanilla extract
- 1 cup boiling water

For the Cherry Filling:

- 2 cans (21 ounces each) cherry pie filling

For the Whipped Cream Frosting:

- 2 cups heavy cream, chilled
- 1/2 cup powdered sugar
- 1 teaspoon vanilla extract

For Garnish:

- Dark chocolate shavings or curls
- Maraschino cherries (optional)

Instructions:

For the Chocolate Cake:

    Preheat Oven:
- Preheat your oven to 350°F (175°C). Grease and flour two 9-inch round cake pans.

Combine Dry Ingredients:
- In a large mixing bowl, sift together the flour, sugar, cocoa powder, baking powder, baking soda, and salt.

Add Wet Ingredients:
- Add the eggs, milk, vegetable oil, and vanilla extract to the dry ingredients. Mix until well combined.

Add Boiling Water:
- Gradually add the boiling water to the batter, mixing well. The batter will be thin, but that's okay.

Pour into Pans:
- Pour the batter evenly into the prepared cake pans.

Bake:
- Bake in the preheated oven for 30-35 minutes or until a toothpick inserted into the center comes out clean.

Cool:
- Allow the cakes to cool in the pans for 10 minutes, then transfer them to a wire rack to cool completely.

For the Whipped Cream Frosting:

Whip Cream:
- In a chilled bowl, whip the heavy cream until soft peaks form.

Add Sugar and Vanilla:
- Gradually add the powdered sugar and vanilla extract. Continue whipping until stiff peaks form. Be careful not to over-whip.

Assemble the Black Forest Cake:

Level Cakes (Optional):
- If needed, level the cooled cakes using a serrated knife or cake leveler.

Place First Cake Layer:
- Place one cake layer on a serving platter or cake stand.

Spread Cherry Filling:
- Spread a layer of cherry pie filling over the top of the first cake layer.

Add Second Cake Layer:
- Place the second cake layer on top, pressing down gently.

Frost with Whipped Cream:
- Frost the entire cake with the whipped cream frosting. Use a spatula to create a smooth finish.

Decorate:
- Decorate the top and sides of the cake with dark chocolate shavings or curls. Optionally, garnish with maraschino cherries.

Serve:

Chill (Optional):
- For best results, chill the Black Forest Cake in the refrigerator for at least 1-2 hours before serving.

Slice and Enjoy:
- Slice and serve this classic Black Forest Cake. Enjoy the combination of rich chocolate, cherries, and light whipped cream.

Tips:

- If you want to enhance the cherry flavor, you can brush each cake layer with a bit of cherry juice before adding the cherry filling.
- Ensure the heavy cream is well chilled for better whipping results.

Indulge in the decadence of this classic Black Forest Cake, perfect for celebrations or special occasions!

Gluten-Free and Vegan Options:
Gluten-Free Chocolate Chip Cookies

Ingredients:

- 1 cup unsalted butter, softened
- 1 cup granulated sugar
- 1 cup brown sugar, packed
- 2 large eggs
- 1 teaspoon vanilla extract
- 2 1/4 cups gluten-free all-purpose flour
- 1/2 teaspoon xanthan gum (omit if your gluten-free flour blend already contains it)
- 1 teaspoon baking soda
- 1/2 teaspoon baking powder
- 1/2 teaspoon salt
- 2 cups gluten-free chocolate chips

Instructions:

Preheat Oven:
- Preheat your oven to 350°F (175°C). Line baking sheets with parchment paper.

Cream Butter and Sugars:
- In a large mixing bowl, cream together the softened butter, granulated sugar, and brown sugar until light and fluffy.

Add Eggs and Vanilla:
- Add the eggs one at a time, beating well after each addition. Stir in the vanilla extract.

Combine Dry Ingredients:
- In a separate bowl, whisk together the gluten-free all-purpose flour, xanthan gum (if needed), baking soda, baking powder, and salt.

Add Dry Ingredients to Wet Ingredients:
- Gradually add the dry ingredients to the butter mixture, mixing until just combined.

Fold in Chocolate Chips:
- Gently fold in the gluten-free chocolate chips until evenly distributed in the cookie dough.

Chill Dough (Optional):
- If time allows, you can chill the cookie dough in the refrigerator for about 30 minutes. This helps prevent cookies from spreading too much during baking.

Scoop Dough onto Baking Sheets:
- Drop rounded tablespoons of cookie dough onto the prepared baking sheets, spacing them about 2 inches apart.

Bake:
- Bake in the preheated oven for 10-12 minutes or until the edges are golden brown. The centers may look slightly undercooked but will continue to set as they cool.

Cool on Baking Sheets:
- Allow the cookies to cool on the baking sheets for 5 minutes, then transfer them to wire racks to cool completely.

Store:
- Store the gluten-free chocolate chip cookies in an airtight container at room temperature.

Tips:

- Ensure that all your ingredients, including the chocolate chips, are labeled gluten-free if you have strict dietary restrictions.
- Experiment with different gluten-free flour blends to find one that works best for your taste and dietary needs.
- If the dough is too sticky, you can refrigerate it for a longer time or add a bit more gluten-free flour until it reaches a manageable consistency.

Enjoy these delicious gluten-free chocolate chip cookies that are perfect for those with gluten sensitivities or for anyone who loves a classic chocolate chip treat!

Vegan Banana Bread

Ingredients:

- 3 to 4 ripe bananas, mashed
- 1/2 cup unsweetened applesauce
- 1/3 cup melted coconut oil or vegetable oil
- 1/2 cup granulated sugar
- 1/2 cup brown sugar, packed
- 1 teaspoon vanilla extract
- 1 3/4 cups all-purpose flour
- 1 teaspoon baking soda
- 1/2 teaspoon baking powder
- 1/2 teaspoon salt
- 1 teaspoon ground cinnamon (optional)
- 1/2 cup chopped nuts or chocolate chips (optional)

Instructions:

Preheat Oven:
- Preheat your oven to 350°F (175°C). Grease or line a standard-sized loaf pan.

Mash Bananas:
- In a large mixing bowl, mash the ripe bananas with a fork until smooth.

Add Wet Ingredients:
- Add the applesauce, melted coconut oil or vegetable oil, granulated sugar, brown sugar, and vanilla extract to the mashed bananas. Mix well to combine.

Combine Dry Ingredients:
- In a separate bowl, whisk together the all-purpose flour, baking soda, baking powder, salt, and ground cinnamon if using.

Combine Wet and Dry Ingredients:
- Gradually add the dry ingredients to the wet ingredients, stirring until just combined. Be careful not to overmix.

Fold in Nuts or Chocolate Chips (Optional):
- If desired, fold in chopped nuts or chocolate chips into the batter.

Pour into Loaf Pan:
- Pour the batter into the prepared loaf pan, spreading it evenly.

Bake:

- Bake in the preheated oven for 55-65 minutes or until a toothpick inserted into the center comes out clean or with a few moist crumbs.

Cool:
- Allow the vegan banana bread to cool in the pan for 10 minutes, then transfer it to a wire rack to cool completely.

Slice and Serve:
- Once completely cooled, slice and serve the vegan banana bread. Enjoy!

Tips:

- Adjust the sweetness by varying the amount of sugar according to your taste preference.
- Add a handful of chopped nuts, such as walnuts or pecans, for added texture.
- For a variation, you can stir in a half cup of dairy-free chocolate chips or raisins into the batter.

This vegan banana bread is a delicious and plant-based alternative to the classic recipe, perfect for breakfast or as a tasty snack.

Gluten-Free Lemon Bars

Ingredients:

For the Crust:

- 1 cup gluten-free all-purpose flour
- 1/2 cup unsalted butter, softened
- 1/4 cup powdered sugar
- Pinch of salt

For the Lemon Filling:

- 1 1/2 cups granulated sugar
- 1/4 cup gluten-free all-purpose flour
- 4 large eggs
- 2/3 cup fresh lemon juice (about 4-5 lemons)
- Zest of 2 lemons
- Powdered sugar for dusting (optional)

Instructions:

For the Crust:

Preheat Oven:
- Preheat your oven to 350°F (175°C). Line a 9x9-inch baking pan with parchment paper, leaving an overhang on two sides for easy removal.

Combine Crust Ingredients:
- In a medium bowl, combine the gluten-free all-purpose flour, softened butter, powdered sugar, and a pinch of salt. Mix until the ingredients come together to form a crumbly dough.

Press into Pan:
- Press the crust mixture into the bottom of the prepared baking pan to create an even layer.

Bake:
- Bake the crust in the preheated oven for 15-20 minutes or until it's lightly golden. Remove from the oven and set aside.

For the Lemon Filling:

- Whisk Filling Ingredients:
  - In a bowl, whisk together the granulated sugar and gluten-free all-purpose flour. Add the eggs, fresh lemon juice, and lemon zest. Whisk until well combined.
- Pour Over Baked Crust:
  - Pour the lemon filling over the pre-baked crust.
- Bake Again:
  - Bake in the oven for 20-25 minutes or until the filling is set and the edges are lightly golden.
- Cool:
  - Allow the gluten-free lemon bars to cool completely in the pan.
- Chill (Optional):
  - For easier cutting, you can chill the lemon bars in the refrigerator for a few hours or overnight.
- Dust with Powdered Sugar (Optional):
  - Before serving, dust the top with powdered sugar if desired.
- Slice and Serve:
  - Use the parchment paper overhang to lift the lemon bars out of the pan. Place on a cutting board and slice into squares.

Tips:

- Ensure that all your ingredients, especially the gluten-free flour, are labeled gluten-free if you have strict dietary restrictions.
- For the lemon juice, fresh is recommended for the best flavor, but you can use bottled lemon juice if needed.

Enjoy these gluten-free lemon bars as a delightful and tangy treat. They're perfect for any occasion and a great addition to your gluten-free dessert options!

Vegan Chocolate Cupcakes

Ingredients:

Dry Ingredients:

- 1 1/2 cups all-purpose flour
- 1 cup granulated sugar
- 1/3 cup cocoa powder
- 1 teaspoon baking soda
- 1/2 teaspoon baking powder
- 1/2 teaspoon salt

Wet Ingredients:

- 1 cup unsweetened almond milk (or any non-dairy milk)
- 1/2 cup vegetable oil (or melted coconut oil)
- 2 teaspoons apple cider vinegar
- 2 teaspoons vanilla extract

For Frosting:

- 1/2 cup vegan butter, softened
- 2 cups powdered sugar
- 1/4 cup cocoa powder
- 2-3 tablespoons non-dairy milk
- 1 teaspoon vanilla extract

Instructions:

Preheat Oven:
- Preheat your oven to 350°F (175°C). Line a muffin tin with cupcake liners.

Combine Dry Ingredients:
- In a large mixing bowl, whisk together the all-purpose flour, granulated sugar, cocoa powder, baking soda, baking powder, and salt.

Combine Wet Ingredients:

- In a separate bowl, whisk together the almond milk, vegetable oil, apple cider vinegar, and vanilla extract.

Combine Wet and Dry Ingredients:
- Pour the wet ingredients into the bowl of dry ingredients. Stir until just combined. Do not overmix.

Fill Cupcake Liners:
- Divide the batter evenly among the cupcake liners, filling each about two-thirds full.

Bake:
- Bake in the preheated oven for 18-20 minutes or until a toothpick inserted into the center comes out clean.

Cool:
- Allow the cupcakes to cool in the muffin tin for 5 minutes, then transfer them to a wire rack to cool completely.

For Frosting:

Beat Vegan Butter:
- In a mixing bowl, beat the softened vegan butter until creamy.

Add Cocoa Powder and Powdered Sugar:
- Sift in the cocoa powder and add the powdered sugar. Beat until well combined.

Add Non-Dairy Milk and Vanilla:
- Add non-dairy milk and vanilla extract. Beat until smooth and creamy. Adjust the consistency by adding more powdered sugar or non-dairy milk if needed.

Frost Cupcakes:
- Once the cupcakes are completely cooled, frost them with the chocolate frosting using a piping bag or a spatula.

Decorate (Optional):
- Decorate the cupcakes with sprinkles, chocolate shavings, or any other toppings of your choice.

Serve and Enjoy:
- Serve and enjoy these delicious vegan chocolate cupcakes!

Tips:

- Make sure the cupcakes are completely cool before frosting to prevent the frosting from melting.
- Feel free to customize the cupcakes by adding vegan chocolate chips to the batter or filling them with a vegan chocolate ganache.
- Adjust the sweetness of the frosting to your liking by adding more or less powdered sugar.

These vegan chocolate cupcakes are a delectable treat for any occasion, and the rich, chocolatey flavor will satisfy any sweet tooth!

Almond Flour Brownies (Gluten-Free)

Ingredients:

- 1 cup almond flour
- 1/2 cup cocoa powder
- 1/2 teaspoon baking soda
- 1/4 teaspoon salt
- 1/2 cup unsalted butter, melted (or coconut oil for a dairy-free option)
- 1 cup granulated sugar
- 2 large eggs
- 1 teaspoon vanilla extract
- 1/2 cup chocolate chips (optional)
- Chopped nuts (optional)

Instructions:

Preheat Oven:
- Preheat your oven to 350°F (175°C). Grease or line an 8x8-inch baking pan with parchment paper.

Mix Dry Ingredients:
- In a bowl, whisk together the almond flour, cocoa powder, baking soda, and salt until well combined.

Melt Butter:
- In a separate bowl, melt the unsalted butter.

Combine Wet Ingredients:
- Add the granulated sugar to the melted butter and mix until well combined. Add the eggs one at a time, beating well after each addition. Stir in the vanilla extract.

Combine Wet and Dry Ingredients:
- Gradually add the dry ingredients to the wet ingredients, mixing until just combined.

Add Chocolate Chips and Nuts (Optional):
- Fold in chocolate chips and chopped nuts if you desire some extra texture and flavor.

Pour into Baking Pan:
- Pour the batter into the prepared baking pan, spreading it evenly.

Bake:

- Bake in the preheated oven for 20-25 minutes or until a toothpick inserted into the center comes out with moist crumbs (not wet batter).

Cool:
- Allow the almond flour brownies to cool completely in the pan.

Slice and Serve:
- Once cooled, lift the brownies out of the pan using the parchment paper overhang, and slice them into squares.

Store:
- Store the brownies in an airtight container at room temperature for up to several days.

Tips:

- Be cautious not to overbake the brownies, as almond flour tends to dry out more quickly than regular flour.
- You can enhance the flavor by adding a touch of instant coffee to the batter.
- Experiment with different mix-ins such as dried fruit, coconut flakes, or a swirl of nut butter.

These almond flour brownies are a delicious gluten-free option, providing a fudgy and rich chocolate experience. Enjoy this treat without sacrificing taste!

Vegan Blueberry Scones

Ingredients:

- 2 cups all-purpose flour
- 1/4 cup granulated sugar
- 1 tablespoon baking powder
- 1/2 teaspoon salt
- 1/2 cup vegan butter, cold and cubed
- 1/2 cup non-dairy milk (such as almond, soy, or coconut)
- 1 teaspoon vanilla extract
- 1 cup fresh or frozen blueberries
- 1 tablespoon non-dairy milk (for brushing)

Instructions:

Preheat Oven:
- Preheat your oven to 400°F (200°C). Line a baking sheet with parchment paper.

Mix Dry Ingredients:
- In a large bowl, whisk together the all-purpose flour, granulated sugar, baking powder, and salt.

Add Cold Vegan Butter:
- Add the cold and cubed vegan butter to the dry ingredients. Use a pastry cutter or your fingers to cut the butter into the flour until the mixture resembles coarse crumbs.

Combine Wet Ingredients:
- In a separate bowl, mix together the non-dairy milk and vanilla extract.

Combine Wet and Dry Ingredients:
- Pour the wet ingredients into the flour-butter mixture. Stir until just combined. Be careful not to overmix.

Add Blueberries:
- Gently fold in the blueberries, being careful not to crush them.

Shape Dough:
- Turn the dough onto a lightly floured surface and gently knead it a few times until it comes together. Pat the dough into a circle about 1-inch thick.

Cut into Triangles:

- Using a sharp knife, cut the dough into 8 wedges (like a pizza). Place the wedges on the prepared baking sheet, leaving some space between them.

Brush with Non-Dairy Milk:
- Brush the tops of the scones with a little non-dairy milk.

Bake:
- Bake in the preheated oven for 15-18 minutes or until the scones are golden brown and cooked through.

Cool:
- Allow the vegan blueberry scones to cool on the baking sheet for a few minutes before transferring them to a wire rack to cool completely.

Serve and Enjoy:
- Once cooled, serve and enjoy your delicious vegan blueberry scones!

Tips:

- For flakier scones, make sure your vegan butter is cold and handle the dough as little as possible.
- If using frozen blueberries, toss them in a little flour before folding them into the dough to prevent excessive bleeding.
- You can glaze the scones with a simple icing made from powdered sugar and non-dairy milk if desired.

These vegan blueberry scones are a delightful and easy-to-make treat perfect for breakfast or afternoon tea. Enjoy the burst of blueberry flavor in every bite!

Gluten-Free Pumpkin Muffins

Ingredients:

- 2 cups gluten-free all-purpose flour
- 1 teaspoon baking powder
- 1/2 teaspoon baking soda
- 1/2 teaspoon salt
- 1 teaspoon ground cinnamon
- 1/2 teaspoon ground nutmeg
- 1/4 teaspoon ground cloves
- 1/4 cup melted coconut oil or vegetable oil
- 1/2 cup packed brown sugar
- 1/4 cup granulated sugar
- 2 large eggs
- 1 cup canned pumpkin puree
- 1 teaspoon vanilla extract
- 1/2 cup unsweetened applesauce

Optional Add-ins:

- 1/2 cup chopped nuts (such as walnuts or pecans)
- 1/2 cup raisins or chocolate chips

Instructions:

Preheat Oven:
- Preheat your oven to 350°F (175°C). Line a muffin tin with paper liners.

Combine Dry Ingredients:
- In a medium bowl, whisk together the gluten-free all-purpose flour, baking powder, baking soda, salt, cinnamon, nutmeg, and cloves. Set aside.

Mix Wet Ingredients:
- In a large bowl, whisk together the melted coconut oil or vegetable oil, brown sugar, granulated sugar, eggs, pumpkin puree, vanilla extract, and applesauce until well combined.

Combine Wet and Dry Ingredients:
- Gradually add the dry ingredients to the wet ingredients, mixing until just combined. Be careful not to overmix.

Add Optional Add-ins:

- If desired, fold in chopped nuts, raisins, or chocolate chips.

Fill Muffin Cups:
- Spoon the batter into the prepared muffin cups, filling each about two-thirds full.

Bake:
- Bake in the preheated oven for 20-25 minutes or until a toothpick inserted into the center of a muffin comes out clean.

Cool:
- Allow the gluten-free pumpkin muffins to cool in the muffin tin for 5 minutes, then transfer them to a wire rack to cool completely.

Serve and Enjoy:
- Once cooled, serve and enjoy these delicious gluten-free pumpkin muffins!

Tips:

- Ensure that your gluten-free flour blend is labeled gluten-free and contains a mix of flours for the best texture.
- Adjust the sweetness by varying the amount of sugar according to your taste preference.
- You can also add a sprinkle of cinnamon-sugar on top of the muffins before baking for extra flavor.

These gluten-free pumpkin muffins are perfect for a fall treat or any time you're craving a delicious and moist pumpkin-flavored snack!

Vegan Chocolate Avocado Cake

Ingredients:

For the Cake:

- 2 cups all-purpose flour
- 1 1/2 cups granulated sugar
- 1/2 cup cocoa powder
- 2 teaspoons baking powder
- 1/2 teaspoon baking soda
- 1/2 teaspoon salt
- 1 ripe avocado, mashed
- 1 1/2 cups non-dairy milk (such as almond or soy)
- 1/2 cup vegetable oil
- 2 teaspoons vanilla extract
- 1 tablespoon apple cider vinegar

For the Chocolate Avocado Frosting:

- 2 ripe avocados, mashed
- 1/2 cup cocoa powder
- 1 cup powdered sugar
- 1 teaspoon vanilla extract
- Pinch of salt

Instructions:

For the Cake:

   Preheat Oven:
- Preheat your oven to 350°F (175°C). Grease and flour two 9-inch round cake pans.

   Mix Dry Ingredients:
- In a large bowl, whisk together the all-purpose flour, granulated sugar, cocoa powder, baking powder, baking soda, and salt.

   Combine Wet Ingredients:

- In a separate bowl, whisk together the mashed avocado, non-dairy milk, vegetable oil, vanilla extract, and apple cider vinegar.

Combine Wet and Dry Ingredients:
- Gradually add the wet ingredients to the dry ingredients, mixing until just combined. Be careful not to overmix.

Divide Batter:
- Divide the batter evenly between the prepared cake pans.

Bake:
- Bake in the preheated oven for 25-30 minutes or until a toothpick inserted into the center of the cakes comes out clean.

Cool:
- Allow the cakes to cool in the pans for 10 minutes, then transfer them to a wire rack to cool completely.

For the Chocolate Avocado Frosting:

Mix Ingredients:
- In a bowl, combine the mashed avocados, cocoa powder, powdered sugar, vanilla extract, and a pinch of salt. Use an electric mixer to beat the ingredients until smooth and creamy.

Frost the Cake:
- Once the cakes are completely cooled, spread a layer of the chocolate avocado frosting on top of one cake layer. Place the second cake layer on top and frost the entire cake with the remaining frosting.

Decorate (Optional):
- Optionally, you can decorate the cake with shaved chocolate, berries, or any other toppings of your choice.

Slice and Serve:
- Slice and serve this delicious and moist vegan chocolate avocado cake.

Tips:

- Ensure that the avocados are ripe and mashed well for a smooth texture in both the cake and frosting.
- Adjust the sweetness of the frosting by adding more or less powdered sugar according to your taste preference.
- This cake pairs well with a scoop of vegan vanilla ice cream or a dollop of dairy-free whipped cream.

Enjoy this decadent and unique Vegan Chocolate Avocado Cake that's both rich in flavor and wonderfully moist!

Coconut Flour Pancakes (Gluten-Free)

Ingredients:

- 1/2 cup coconut flour
- 1/2 teaspoon baking powder
- Pinch of salt
- 4 large eggs
- 1 cup coconut milk (or any non-dairy milk)
- 2 tablespoons coconut oil, melted
- 1 tablespoon maple syrup (optional, for sweetness)
- 1 teaspoon vanilla extract

Instructions:

Mix Dry Ingredients:
- In a bowl, whisk together the coconut flour, baking powder, and a pinch of salt.

Combine Wet Ingredients:
- In a separate bowl, whisk together the eggs, coconut milk, melted coconut oil, maple syrup (if using), and vanilla extract.

Combine Wet and Dry Ingredients:
- Gradually add the wet ingredients to the dry ingredients, stirring until well combined. Let the batter sit for a couple of minutes to allow the coconut flour to absorb the liquids.

Preheat Griddle or Pan:
- Preheat a griddle or non-stick pan over medium-low heat. Lightly grease the surface with coconut oil or cooking spray.

Scoop Batter onto Griddle:
- Scoop about 1/4 cup of batter onto the griddle for each pancake. Use the back of a spoon to spread the batter into a round shape if needed.

Cook Until Bubbles Form:
- Cook the pancakes until bubbles form on the surface, and the edges start to look set. This will take about 2-3 minutes.

Flip and Cook Other Side:
- Carefully flip the pancakes and cook the other side for an additional 1-2 minutes, or until golden brown.

Repeat:

- Repeat the process with the remaining batter, adding more coconut oil to the griddle as needed.

Serve:
- Serve the coconut flour pancakes warm with your favorite toppings, such as fresh fruit, maple syrup, or coconut whipped cream.

Tips:

- Coconut flour absorbs a lot of liquid, so the batter may seem thick at first. If it becomes too thick as it sits, you can add a little more coconut milk to achieve the desired consistency.
- Keep the heat on the lower side to prevent the pancakes from burning, as coconut flour pancakes can cook quickly.
- Customize your pancakes by adding extras like blueberries, chocolate chips, or chopped nuts to the batter.

Enjoy these fluffy and gluten-free Coconut Flour Pancakes for a delicious and nutritious breakfast or brunch option!

Vegan Almond Joy Energy Bites

Ingredients:

- 1 cup rolled oats
- 1/2 cup almond butter
- 1/4 cup maple syrup
- 1/4 cup shredded coconut (plus extra for coating)
- 1/4 cup chopped almonds
- 1/4 cup dairy-free chocolate chips
- 1 teaspoon vanilla extract
- Pinch of salt

Instructions:

Combine Dry Ingredients:
- In a large mixing bowl, combine rolled oats, shredded coconut, chopped almonds, dairy-free chocolate chips, and a pinch of salt.

Add Wet Ingredients:
- Add almond butter, maple syrup, and vanilla extract to the dry ingredients.

Mix Well:
- Mix all the ingredients thoroughly until well combined. The mixture should be sticky enough to hold together.

Chill:
- Place the mixture in the refrigerator for about 30 minutes. Chilling will make it easier to handle and shape into energy bites.

Shape into Bites:
- After chilling, take the mixture and shape it into bite-sized balls using your hands.

Coat with Shredded Coconut:
- Roll each energy bite in shredded coconut, ensuring they are evenly coated.

Store:
- Place the Almond Joy Energy Bites in an airtight container and refrigerate for longer shelf life.

Serve and Enjoy:
- Enjoy these vegan Almond Joy Energy Bites as a delicious and energy-boosting snack!

Tips:

- Customize your energy bites by adding extras like chia seeds, flaxseeds, or dried fruit.
- Adjust the sweetness by adding more or less maple syrup according to your taste preference.
- If the mixture is too dry, you can add a little more almond butter or maple syrup. If it's too wet, add more oats.

These vegan Almond Joy Energy Bites are a delightful treat that combines the flavors of almonds, coconut, and chocolate in a convenient and energizing snack. Perfect for satisfying your sweet cravings in a healthier way!